ETHICS AND
PROFESSIONAL CONDUCT

The
University of
Law

ETHICS AND
PROFESSIONAL CONDUCT
FIFTH EDITION

Jacqueline Kempton

This edition published 2025 by

The University of Law
2 Bunhill Row
London EC1Y 8HQ

Contains public sector information licensed under the Open Government Licence v3.0

British Library Cataloguing in Publication Data

A catalogue record for this book is available from the British Library.

ISBN 978 1 80502 266 4

Preface

This book is part of a series of Study Manuals that have been specially designed to support the reader to achieve the SQE1 Assessment Specification in relation to Functioning Legal Knowledge. Each Study Manual aims to provide the reader with a solid knowledge and understanding of fundamental legal principles and rules, including how those principles and rules might be applied in practice.

This Study Manual covers the Solicitors Regulation Authority's syllabus for the SQE1 assessment for Ethics and Professional Conduct in a concise and tightly focused manner. The Manual provides a clear statement of relevant legal rules and a well-defined road map through examinable law and practice. The Manual aims to bring the law and practice to life through the use of example scenarios based on realistic client-based problems and allows the reader to test their knowledge and understanding through single best answer questions that have been modelled on the SRA's sample assessment questions.

For those readers who are students at the University of Law, the Study Manual is used alongside other learning resources and the University's assessment bank to best prepare students not only for the SQE1 assessments, but also for a future life in professional legal practice.

We hope that you find the Study Manual supportive of your preparation for SQE1 and we wish you every success.

The legal principles and rules contained within this Manual are stated as at 1 May 2025.

Contents

Table of Cases

Table of Legislation, Codes and Rules

1 Ethics and Regulation

SQE1 syllabus

This chapter will help you to achieve the SQE1 Assessment Specification in relation to Functioning Legal Knowledge concerned with Ethics and Professional Conduct on:

- the purpose, scope and content of the SRA Code of Conduct for Solicitors, RELs and RFLs.

Ethics and Professional Conduct is a pervasive topic in SQE1 and may be examined across all subject areas.

Note that for SQE1, candidates are not usually required to recall specific case names or cite statutory or regulatory authorities. Cases are provided for illustrative purposes only.

Learning outcomes

By the end of this chapter you will be able to demonstrate your ability to act honestly and with integrity, and in accordance with the SRA Standards and Regulations in relation to:

- ethical behaviour;
- regulation of the profession; and
- complaints handling.

1.1 Introduction

Solicitors are expected to meet high standards of ethical behaviour. Those standards are reflected in the manner in which the profession is regulated. 'Professional conduct' is the term that is often used to describe the rules and regulations with which a solicitor must comply. Solicitors, like every other person, must comply with the laws of the country. However, additional requirements are placed upon solicitors due to the nature of their work.

This chapter looks at:

- ethics
- the Solicitors Regulation Authority
- complaints
- the Legal Ombudsman
- breach of professional conduct
- the Solicitors Disciplinary Tribunal
- powers of the court
- negligence
- the Solicitors Compensation Fund.

1.2 Ethics

On its website page 'Ethics', The Law Society says:

The commitment to behaving ethically is at the heart of what it means to be a solicitor.

In essence ethics is a system of moral principles or values governing how people behave. In other words, behaving ethically means 'doing the right thing'.

'Ethical' is not synonymous with 'legal'. Behaviour can be unethical without being illegal, for example committing adultery. However, there are obvious overlaps. Breaking the law will often also constitute unethical conduct.

It goes without saying that solicitors are required to follow the same ethical principles that apply to everyone. For example, solicitors, in common with everyone else, are expected to refrain from killing innocent people. However, it is generally accepted that solicitors are subject to additional ethical obligations. In *Law Society (Solicitors Regulation Authority) v Emeana and others* [2013] EWHC 2130 (Admin) Lord Justice Moses said: 'I do not believe that the public would find it acceptable that those who have behaved in this way should be allowed to act as solicitors.' This indicates that society expects something more from solicitors or that solicitors are expected to adopt higher standards of ethical behaviour.

It may also be that general ethical principles apply differently to solicitors. For example, a member of the public who knew that an individual had committed a crime would be expected to report the perpetrator to the police. However, for a solicitor, if the perpetrator is a client, then the duty of client confidentiality may mean that the solicitor is not under the same obligation to report the matter.

The particular expectations placed on solicitors to behave ethically arise because solicitors have a special relationship with their clients and a special place within the justice system. Clients must have total confidence that their solicitor will behave ethically in dealing with the personal information and valuable assets that the client will entrust to them. By the same token, if an individual solicitor acts unethically this taints the justice system as a whole, with the result that public trust in that system declines.

There are many theories surrounding ethics and the approach to be adopted in resolving ethical dilemmas. These are beyond the scope of this manual. Such theories, however, have influenced the regulation of the profession which, at heart, seeks to maintain ethical behaviour. Suffice it to say that the approach has changed over the years. Traditionally, the approach was character based in that it was thought that the innate moral compass of the solicitor would enable them to act ethically or honourably. In the more recent past, a rules-based approach was adopted so that the right ethical response was established by strict adherence to a detailed set of rules.

Today, the focus is on the consequences of behaviour. In other words, the ethical approach is the one which produces the best outcome. But that does not mean that the ethical approach will be easy to ascertain or that there will be a single answer. There are core standards to be applied, but there is also flexibility. Personal judgment must be applied and the individual facts of the case considered. In many ways the joint application of core standards and personal judgment should point a solicitor to choosing a path of action that will produce the most good (or the least harm).

Ethics underpins the regulation of the profession. As the Solicitors' Regulation Authority says,

> As well as making sure solicitors are competent, we want to promote a culture where ethical values and behaviours are embedded.

1.3 The Solicitors Regulation Authority

The Solicitors Regulation Authority (SRA) regulates solicitors, the bodies in which they operate and all those working within those bodies. As part of its regulatory function, the SRA publishes and enforces rules governing how solicitors behave and conduct their business. The rules are contained in the SRA Standards and Regulations. Those regulated by the SRA must comply with these Standards and Regulations, and the SRA may exercise its powers to take action against those who fail to do so.

The SRA Standards and Regulations deal with a variety of regulatory matters. Key elements are:

1.3.1 The SRA Principles

These set out the fundamental requirements of ethical behaviour which must be upheld by all those regulated by the SRA. The Principles underpin the Standards and Regulations.

1.3.2 The SRA Code of Conduct for Solicitors, RELs and RFLs ('Code of Conduct for Solicitors')

This sets out the standards of professionalism required from the individuals (solicitors, registered European lawyers and registered foreign lawyers) authorised by the SRA to provide legal services. The introduction to the Code indicates that such individuals are personally accountable for compliance with the Code. The individual must exercise their own judgment in applying the standards to the situations they are in and deciding on a course of action, taking into account factors such as their roles and responsibilities, areas of practice and nature of their clients.

1.3.3 The SRA Code of Conduct for Firms

This sets out the standards and business controls expected of firms (including sole practices) authorised by the SRA to provide legal services. The introduction to the Code indicates that a serious failure to meet its standards may lead to the SRA taking regulatory action against the body itself as an entity, or its managers or compliance officers. It may also take action against employees working within the body for any breaches for which they are responsible. Many of the rules in the Code of Conduct for Solicitors are replicated in or incorporated into the Code of Conduct for Firms.

The Code of Conduct for Solicitors and the Code of Conduct for Firms are known collectively as the Code of Conduct.

1.3.4 The SRA Accounts Rules

These detail specific requirements placed on solicitors in financial matters, in particular when dealing with money belonging to clients or third parties. The content of these Rules is beyond the scope of this manual.

1.3.5 The SRA Glossary

This contains all the defined terms (which appear in italics in the text) from the Codes, Rules and Regulations.

For ease of reference, in this manual the terms 'solicitor' and 'firm' will be used, although from the above it is clear that the reach of the SRA Standards and Regulations is wider. All references to 'Principle' are to the SRA Principles and references to 'Paragraph' are to the Code of Conduct for Solicitors unless stated otherwise.

From time to time the SRA issues Guidance to supplement the SRA Standards and Regulations.

The SRA Standards and Regulations are underpinned by the SRA Enforcement Strategy. Not every breach of the rules will result in an investigation being undertaken or sanctions being imposed by the SRA. The SRA's focus is on behaviour or breaches which it considers to be 'serious'. The Enforcement Strategy explains how the SRA assesses the seriousness of the conduct and the approach it takes towards the imposing of sanctions (see **10.6**).

The SRA is entirely separate from the Law Society. The Law Society is the representative body for solicitors in England and Wales.

1.4 Complaints

Complaints from some clients about the legal service they have received are perhaps inevitable. A complaint may be made about something which happens, or fails to happen, during the conduct of the client's matter, or arises at the end when the client is dissatisfied with the outcome. Some complaints will be justified, others not. Some complaints will involve allegations of professional misconduct, others not. Dealing with all complaints appropriately is part and parcel of delivering a professional service. The Code of Conduct for Solicitors contains some specific requirements in respect of complaints handling.

A solicitor must either establish and maintain, or participate in, a procedure for handling complaints in relation to the legal services they provide (Paragraph 8.2).

A solicitor must ensure (Paragraph 8.3) that clients are informed in writing at the time of engagement about:

(a) their right to complain about the solicitor's services and charges;

(b) how complaints may be made and to whom; and

(c) any right they have to make a complaint to the Legal Ombudsman (see **1.5**) and when they can make such complaint.

Under the SRA Transparency Rules, certain information about complaints procedures must be published on a firm's website, or be made available on request if the firm has no website (see **3.3.3.4**).

Many complaints will be resolved using the firm's own complaints procedure. In most cases a dissatisfied client should use this procedure first, before taking more formal action.

When a client has made a complaint, if this has not been resolved to the client's satisfaction within eight weeks following the making of a complaint, the solicitor must ensure (Paragraph 8.4) that the client is informed in writing:

(a) of any right they have to complain to the Legal Ombudsman, the timeframe for doing so and full details of how to contact the Legal Ombudsman; and

(b) if a complaint has been brought and the complaints procedure has been exhausted:

   (i) that the solicitor cannot settle the complaint;

   (ii) the name and website address of an alternative dispute resolution (ADR) approved body which would be competent to deal with the complaint; and

   (iii) whether the solicitor agrees to use the scheme operated by that body.

The Chartered Trading Standards Institute has approved a number of ADR entities that will be able to provide ADR services. The obligation placed on the solicitor is to provide information about an ADR-approved body and to indicate whether the solicitor is agreeable to using it, and so the client is not required to submit the complaint to the body unless the client wishes to.

Clients' complaints must be dealt with promptly, fairly and free of charge (Paragraph 8.5).

1.5   The Legal Ombudsman

The Legal Ombudsman for England and Wales ('LeO') deals with complaints made against solicitors, barristers, legal executives, licensed conveyancers, notaries and patent attorneys (amongst others).

The LeO (rather than the SRA) will usually be the first point of contact for a client with a complaint about their solicitor or the legal service they have received. The client does not have to suffer any loss for the LeO to make a determination against the solicitor arising from a complaint about the services provided. The mere fact that the solicitor has provided services which are not of the quality reasonably to be expected of a solicitor is enough.

The Scheme Rules provide that only certain types of client can complain to the LeO, including individuals, 'micro-enterprises' (broadly speaking, an enterprise with fewer than 10 staff and a turnover or balance sheet value not exceeding €2 million), charities, clubs and associations with an annual income net of tax of less than £1 million, and personal representatives or beneficiaries of a person's estate. The complaint must relate to an act/omission by the solicitor and must relate to the services which the solicitor provided. The LeO also accepts complaints in relation to services which the solicitor offered, provided or refused to provide to the complainant.

Ordinarily, the complainant cannot use the LeO unless the solicitor's own complaints procedure has been used, but can do so if:

(a) the complaint has not been resolved to the complainant's satisfaction within eight weeks of being made to the solicitor; or

(b) the LeO considers that there are exceptional reasons to consider the complaint sooner, or without it having been made first to the solicitor; or

(c) the LeO considers that in-house resolution is not possible due to irretrievable breakdown in the relationship between the solicitor and the complainant.

The complaint should be brought no later than:

- one year from the act/omission; or

- one year from when the complainant should reasonably have known there was cause for complaint.

However, the LeO has a discretion to extend the time limits to the extent it considers fair.

When the LeO accepts a complaint for investigation, it aims to resolve it by whatever means it considers appropriate, including informal resolution. If the LeO considers that an investigation is necessary, both parties will be given an opportunity to make representations. A hearing will be held only where the LeO considers that the complaint cannot be determined fairly without one. A 'determination' will then be made and sent to the parties and the SRA (as the approved regulator), with a time-limit for response by the complainant. Once the complainant accepts or rejects the determination (or fails to respond), the solicitor and the SRA will be notified of the outcome. The details of the procedure are set out in the Scheme Rules.

The LeO's determination may direct the solicitor (or their firm) to:

(a) apologise;

(b) pay compensation (together with interest) for any loss suffered and/or inconvenience/ distress caused;

(c) ensure (and pay for) the putting right of any error or omission;

(d) take (and pay for) any specified action in the interests of the complainant;

(e) pay a specified amount for the costs of the complainant in pursuing the complaint;

(f) limit the solicitor's fees (including requiring that all or part of any amount paid is refunded, with or without interest, or that all or part of the fees are remitted).

The determination may contain one or more of the above directions. There is a limit of £50,000 on the total value that may be awarded in respect of compensation and the costs in respect of (c) and (d) above. The limit does not apply to (a), (e) or (f) above, or to interest on compensation for loss suffered.

If the complainant accepts the determination, it is binding on the parties and final, and neither party may start or continue any legal proceedings in respect of the subject matter of the complaint. It may be enforced through the High Court or county court by the complainant, and the report may also be published. If the complainant rejects the determination, both parties remain free to pursue other legal remedies (such as suing for negligence).

Although the LeO has the power to adjudicate on acts/omissions as a result of which the complainant has suffered loss, in the event that the LeO considers that the resolution of a particular legal question is necessary in order to resolve a dispute, it may refer that question to the court.

Where the LeO receives a complaint which discloses any alleged professional misconduct on the part of the solicitor, it will inform the SRA.

1.6 Breach of professional conduct

1.6.1 Professional misconduct

'Professional misconduct' primarily concerns breaches of the SRA's Principles and/or the Codes of Conduct. For example, if a solicitor gave an undertaking (see **Chapter 8**) to post the client's witness statement to another solicitor on 1 May and then failed to do so, the solicitor would not have complied with Paragraph 1.3 (the obligation to perform undertakings) and so would be said to breach the requirements of professional conduct.

1.6.2 The role of the SRA

Although complaints from the general public are received through the LeO, complaints primarily concerning a breach of professional conduct will go on to be dealt with by the SRA.

Primarily, the role of the SRA is to protect the public. Accordingly, having received an allegation that a solicitor has committed professional misconduct or committed, or is responsible for, a serious breach of any of the SRA's regulatory obligations, the SRA will decide whether or not to carry out an investigation. The SRA makes the decision by applying its three step Assessment Threshold Test: (1) has there been a potential breach of the SRA Standards and Regulations based on the allegations made; (2) is that potential breach sufficiently serious that, if proved, is capable of regulatory action; (3) is the breach capable of proof? If the SRA decides to carry out an investigation, it will inform the individual or firm about whom the allegation has been made and their employer (where relevant). Notice will be given to that individual or firm setting out the allegation and facts in support and other relevant information and inviting them to respond with written recommendations within a specified time period.

In order to investigate complaints of misconduct, the SRA has the power, under s 44B Solicitors Act 1974, to serve a notice on a solicitor requiring the delivery of a file or documents in the possession of the solicitor to the SRA. Paragraph 7.4 imposes an obligation to respond promptly to the SRA and provide information and documents in response to any such request.

The powers of the SRA following a finding of professional misconduct depend upon the subject of the complaint. The more serious the misconduct, the more severe the sanction.

The SRA's approach is set out in the SRA Enforcement Strategy (see **1.3** and **10.6**). The SRA may impose sanctions (intended to discipline the individual) or controls (intended to protect the public). Examples of action which may be taken by the SRA include:

(a) *Take no further action with or without issuing advice or a warning about future conduct*

The SRA may decide at any stage that no further action is necessary and, in doing so, may decide to issue advice to the individual against whom the allegation was made or issue a warning to them about their future conduct or behaviour. This may be appropriate to respond to a minor regulatory breach which does not require action to protect the public/public interest and is not sufficiently serious to require action to restrict the individual's ability to practise or to rebuke or impose a financial penalty.

(b) *Impose a financial penalty or written rebuke*

The maximum financial penalty for solicitors is £25,000. The SRA has a fixed penalty scheme for specified breaches by firms, eg a failure to provide information or documents to the SRA when requested. Under the scheme the penalty is £750 for a first breach and £1,500 for a continuation of that breach or a subsequent breach of the same kind.

(c) *Control how the solicitor practises*

The SRA may impose conditions on, or suspend, a solicitor's practising certificate, or make an order to control the person's activities in connection with legal practice. It may also impose conditions on, revoke or suspend the terms and conditions of authorisation of a firm.

(d) *Refer the matter to the Solicitors Disciplinary Tribunal*

In some cases, the SRA does not make a final decision but refers alleged misconduct to the Solicitors Disciplinary Tribunal (see **1.7**), where it is responsible for prosecuting the matter. Essentially, such a referral will be made where the SRA considers that its own powers are not sufficient to deal with the matter. For example, only the Solicitors Disciplinary Tribunal has the power to take the most severe sanction of striking the solicitor off the roll. The SRA's fining powers are currently limited to £25,000. This represents a substantial increase on the pre-July 2022 limit and has enabled the SRA to deal with a broader range of cases itself rather than having to refer them on. In a joint statement with the Solicitors Disciplinary Tribunal issued in January 2023, the SRA said that referrals are likely to be reserved for the most serious cases of individual professional misconduct and those involving unusual aspects, such as allegations of sexual misconduct, misappropriation of client money or where there is likely to be high public interest.

Any of the decisions set out in (b) to (d) above may be made by agreement between the SRA and the individual in question.

The SRA makes its regulatory decisions public. This allows the general public to search under the name of the solicitor they propose to use, to establish whether the solicitor has been subject to any regulatory sanction.

1.7   The Solicitors Disciplinary Tribunal

The Solicitors Disciplinary Tribunal (SDT) hears and determines applications relating to allegations of unbefitting conduct and/or breaches of the requirements of professional conduct by a number of legal service providers, including solicitors. The vast majority of applications to the SDT are made on behalf of the SRA. The SRA may make an application when it is satisfied that there is a realistic prospect of the SDT making an order in respect of the allegation and it is in the public interest to make the application. However, except where the Solicitors Act 1974 expressly provides otherwise, any person may make an application directly to the SDT without first making a complaint to the SRA.

The SDT is independent of both the Law Society and the SRA. The members of the Disciplinary Tribunal are appointed by the Master of the Rolls.

1.7.1   Procedure

The SDT has power to make rules governing its procedure and practice. These rules are made with the concurrence of the Master of the Rolls. The SRA maintains a panel of solicitors in private practice who prosecute applications before the SDT on its behalf. In most cases, either the SRA's own advocates or the panel solicitor will present the case before the SDT. In complex cases, counsel may be instructed to present the case. The SDT does not have powers of investigation nor will it collect evidence itself.

An application to the SDT must be made in the prescribed form, supported by evidence (this will be prepared by the panel solicitor, or the SRA's advocate where the applicant is the SRA). The SDT will consider the application and, if satisfied that there is a case to answer, will fix a hearing date. Either party may be represented at the hearing by a solicitor or counsel. Evidence is given on oath and witnesses may be called.

The decisions of the SDT are called 'Judgments' and 'Orders'. The Order itself, together with brief reasons for the decision, is made available at the end of the hearing. The Order takes effect once it is filed with the Law Society. A detailed written Judgment containing reasons, findings and repeating the Order is made available to the parties, the Law Society and on the SDT website after the hearing (usually within seven weeks of the hearing).

Where (unusually) an application is made directly to the SDT, the SDT may refer the matter to the SRA for investigation before proceeding with the application. Where in such a case the SRA investigates the complaint and finds it to be substantiated, it may take over the application on the applicant's behalf (or deal with the matter by using the powers of the SRA).

1.7.2   Powers of the SDT

Section 47 Solicitors Act 1974 gives the SDT power to make such order as in its discretion it thinks fit, including the following:

(a) striking a solicitor off the roll (once struck off the SDT may also restore a solicitor to the roll);

(b) suspending a solicitor from practice or imposing restrictions upon the way in which a solicitor can practise;

(c) imposing an unlimited fine payable to HM Treasury;

(d) reprimanding the solicitor;

(e) requiring the payment by any party of costs or a contribution towards costs.

An appeal from a substantive decision of the Disciplinary Tribunal is made to the Administrative Court.

1.8 Powers of the court

A solicitor is an officer of the court. Accordingly, the court has jurisdiction to discipline the solicitor in respect of costs within any matter before the court. The court may order the solicitor to pay costs to their own client, or to a third party (Civil Procedure Rules, rr 44 and 45).

1.9 Negligence

A solicitor owes a duty of care to the client in the law of tort. Where the solicitor breaches this duty and the client suffers loss as a result, the solicitor may be sued by the client for negligence.

The LeO and the SRA have no power to adjudicate upon issues of negligence in a legal sense. They are not courts and so do not have the power to adjudicate on legal issues. However, there may be an overlap between negligence and complaints about professional services. For example, a solicitor may miss a deadline in respect of issuing proceedings, which would then deprive the client of the opportunity to pursue the matter in court. The service provided would clearly be below what is reasonable to expect from a solicitor. However, it would also constitute negligence, as the solicitor has breached the duty of care to the client and as a result the client has suffered a foreseeable loss (ie the client will not be able to pursue the matter in court and recover damages). Consequently, in addition to or instead of the actions that the SRA or Legal Ombudsman may take, a solicitor may be sued by their client in the tort of negligence.

A solicitor must be 'honest and open' with clients if things go wrong, and if a client suffers loss or harm as a result, matters are to be put right (if possible) and a full and prompt explanation given as to what has happened and the likely impact. If requested to do so by the SRA, a solicitor must investigate whether anyone may have a claim against them, provide the SRA with a report on the outcome of the investigation and notify relevant persons that they may have such a claim accordingly (Paragraph 7.11).

In circumstances where the client notifies the solicitor of their intention to make a claim, or where the solicitor discovers an act or omission which might give rise to a claim, consideration must be given as to whether a conflict (see **Chapter 7**) has arisen and/or whether the client should be advised to obtain independent advice. It will be very rare that a conflict of interest does not arise in such a situation. However, The Law Society's guidance states that solicitors should respond to complaints even if they believe the allegations concern negligence and a referral to the firm's insurance provider will be necessary.

Where the solicitor does cease to act for the client, and is asked to hand over the papers to another solicitor who is giving independent advice on the merits of a claim, the solicitor should keep copies of the original documents for their own reference.

1.10 The SRA Compensation Fund

The SRA Compensation Fund is maintained by the SRA. The Fund is governed by the SRA Compensation Fund Rules and exists as a discretionary fund of last resort to make grants to persons whose money has been stolen or otherwise not accounted for as the result of an act or omission of those regulated by the SRA, and to relieve losses for which SRA-authorised bodies should have had insurance but did not. It is funded by mandatory contributions by all solicitors and SRA-authorised bodies. Applications to this Fund may be made where an individual/organisation has suffered loss due to a defaulting practitioner's dishonesty, or where the individual/organisation is suffering loss and hardship due to a defaulting practitioner's failure to account for monies they have received. The term 'defaulting practitioner' includes a solicitor.

Eligibility criteria setting out those applicants that may be able to apply for a grant are set out in the SRA Compensation Fund Rules. Individuals/organisations are not automatically entitled to a grant from the Fund (they have to apply, and their claims will be assessed). The Fund does not pay out sums of more than £2 million per claim (unless the SRA is satisfied that there are exceptional circumstances in the public interest that justify a higher sum). Where there are multiple related or connected claims, the SRA may impose a cap of £5 million on the total amount paid.

Where payment is made from the Fund, the SRA will seek to be subrogated to the rights of the applicant and can therefore take proceedings against the defaulting solicitor to recover the amount paid out of the Fund. The client may be asked to exhaust any legal remedy before applying to the Fund.

The Code of Conduct for Solicitors imposes an obligation on solicitors to ensure that clients understand the regulatory protections available to them, and this will include eligibility to claim under the Fund (Paragraph 8.11).

Summary

- Solicitors must meet high ethical standards.

- The SRA is empowered by the Solicitors Act 1974 to publish rules and requirements for the regulation of conduct of, amongst others, solicitors.

- These rules and requirements are enforced by the SRA and the Legal Ombudsman.

- The SRA deals with breaches of the requirements of professional conduct, whereas the Legal Ombudsman primarily deals with complaints about services provided by legal practitioners, including solicitors.

- The Legal Ombudsman deals with complaints relating to an act/omission by a legal practitioner and which relates to services provided by the solicitor. The client does not need to suffer any loss as a result of the service provided in order to raise the issue.

- The SRA may impose disciplinary sanctions for a breach of the requirements of professional conduct, or in serious cases may refer the matter to the Solicitors Disciplinary Tribunal.

- The Legal Ombudsman has numerous sanctions at its disposal. These include directing the solicitor to limit their fees, or directing the solicitor to compensate the client up to £50,000. The SRA/Legal Ombudsman has no power to pay compensation to the client itself.

- The Solicitors Disciplinary Tribunal may fine a solicitor, suspend the solicitor or, as an ultimate sanction, strike the solicitor off the roll.

- A solicitor will be negligent if they breach the duty of care to the client and foreseeable loss results as a consequence of that breach. Where the solicitor has been negligent, they may be sued by the client for damages.

- The SRA Compensation Fund is maintained by the SRA. Payment may be made from the Fund when a client has suffered loss as a result of a defaulting practitioner's act or omission or to cover claims against uninsured firms.

Sample questions

Question 1

A client has complained about the manner in which a junior solicitor dealt with their case. In accordance with the firm's complaints procedure, the complaint has been passed to the senior partner for investigation. The senior partner has a very heavy caseload and has not been able to consider the complaint. After several weeks, having heard nothing from the senior partner or the firm, the client takes the complaint to the Legal Ombudsman. The Legal Ombudsman finds that the original complaint is unjustified.

What action can the Legal Ombudsman take?

A   The Legal Ombudsman can take no further action against the senior partner or the firm.

B   The Legal Ombudsman may require the firm to pay compensation to the client but can take no further action with regard to the senior partner personally.

C   The Legal Ombudsman can both require the firm to pay compensation to the client and report the senior partner to the SRA.

D   The only action that the Legal Ombudsman can take is to ask the firm to apologise for the delay in dealing with the complaint.

E   The Legal Ombudsman may report the senior partner to the SRA but can take no further action with regard to the firm.

Answer

Option C is correct. Although the complaint was unjustified, it has not been dealt with properly and so the Legal Ombudsman may still take action, including requiring the client to be compensated for inconvenience and so on. The senior partner is in breach of Paragraph 8.5 because the complaint has not been dealt with promptly and the Legal Ombudsman may report the senior partner to the SRA for that reason.

Question 2

A solicitor is acting for a client in a litigation matter. Whilst the solicitor is presenting the client's case at the final hearing, the solicitor forgets to refer to a recently decided case that would help the client's case. Consequently, the judge finds in favour of the opponent.

Which of the following best explains the solicitor's duties in this situation?

A   The solicitor must not tell the client about the failure to refer to the recent case because that would risk bringing the firm's name into disrepute.

B   The solicitor is under no obligation to tell the client about the failure to refer to the recent case because the client has not yet indicated that they intend to bring a claim for negligence.

C   The solicitor is under no obligation to tell the client about the failure to refer to the recent case because any loss to the client will be covered by the firm's insurance.

D   The solicitor has a duty to be open and honest with the client and so must immediately tell the client about the failure to refer to the recent case.

E   The solicitor has a duty to be open and honest with the client, but should delay telling the client about the failure to refer to the recent case until the solicitor has discussed the matter with the firm's senior partner.

Answer

Option D is correct. Paragraph 7.9 requires a solicitor to be open and honest if things go wrong so the solicitor should tell the client about the omission immediately. The duty is not dependent on the client intending to bring a claim against the solicitor. There is no justification for delay. It is irrelevant that the firm's reputation may be damaged or that any claim would be covered by insurance.

Question 3

A solicitor is instructed by a new client. In conversation at the first interview the solicitor explains that the client has a right to complain about the solicitor's services and charges; how complaints may be made and to whom; and that the client has a right to make a complaint to the Legal Ombudsman and when such a complaint could be made. The solicitor says that they will send a letter to the client confirming the information. However, the solicitor forgets to send the letter.

A few days later the solicitor receives a letter from the client, alleging that at the interview the solicitor had been rude and made a sexist remark. In accordance with the firm's complaints procedure the solicitor hands the letter to the firm's senior partner. The client's allegations about the solicitor are untrue.

Did the solicitor breach the SRA Code of Conduct for Solicitors, RELs and RFLs?

A   No, because the solicitor followed the firm's complaints procedure.

B   No, because the solicitor provided the client with all the information about complaints required by the Code.

C   No, because the solicitor was not rude and did not make a sexist remark.

D   Yes, because the client is unhappy with the legal services they have received.

E   Yes, because the solicitor did not provide the information about complaints in writing.

Answer

Option E is correct. The solicitor acted correctly at the interview and properly complied with the complaints procedure. The solicitor provided all the required information about costs, but, in breach of Paragraph 8.3 did not provide that information in writing. The fact that the client is unhappy does not of itself place the solicitor in breach of the Code.

2 SRA Principles

SQE1 syllabus

This chapter will help you to achieve the SQE1 Assessment Specification in relation to Functioning Legal Knowledge concerned with Ethics and Professional Conduct on:

- the purpose, scope and content of the SRA Principles.

Ethics and Professional Conduct is a pervasive topic in SQE1 and may be examined across all subject areas.

Note that for SQE1, candidates are not usually required to recall specific case names or cite statutory or regulatory authorities. Cases are provided for illustrative purposes only.

Learning outcomes

By the end of this chapter you will be able to demonstrate your ability to act honestly and with integrity, and in accordance with the SRA Standards and Regulations in relation to:

- the core requirements of the SRA Principles.

2.1 Introduction

The SRA Standards and Regulations begin with the SRA Principles. These Principles define the fundamental ethical and professional standards that the SRA expects of all firms and individuals it regulates. The Principles are all-pervasive and underpin all of the SRA's regulatory arrangements. The Principles are therefore a starting point for any consideration of a solicitor's professional conduct responsibilities.

This chapter looks at:

- an overview of the Principles
- justice and the rule of law
- public trust
- independence
- honesty
- integrity
- equality, diversity and inclusion
- best interests of the client.

2.2 An overview of the Principles

The importance of the Principles is evident from the introduction contained in the SRA Standards and Regulations. This states that:

> The SRA Principles comprise the fundamental tenets of ethical behaviour that we expect all those we regulate to uphold.

The Principles are mandatory and apply to all individuals and bodies regulated by the SRA, whether traditional firms of solicitors, ABSs or in-house. They apply outside a solicitor's practice as well as within it and, if not met, are likely to give rise to action being taken by the SRA in accordance with its Enforcement Strategy (see **1.3** and **10.6**).

The Principles are as follows:

> You act:

> (a) in a way that upholds the constitutional principle of the rule of law, and the proper administration of justice;

> (b) in a way that upholds public trust and confidence in the solicitors' profession and in legal services provided by authorised persons;

> (c) with independence;

> (d) with honesty;

> (e) with integrity;

> (f) in a way that encourages equality, diversity and inclusion;

> (g) in the best interests of each client.

In the event that the Principles come into conflict, the introduction makes it clear that it is those Principles that safeguard the wider public interest (such as the rule of law, and public confidence in the profession) which take precedence over the interests of an individual client. Consequently, clients should be made aware that there may be circumstances in which the solicitor's wider professional duties outweigh the solicitor's duty to the individual.

2.3 Justice and the rule of law

Principle 1 requires a solicitor to act in a way that upholds the constitutional principle of the rule of law, and the proper administration of justice.

A breach of Principle 1 may occur in a number of circumstances. The most obvious example is where a solicitor commits a criminal offence. The SRA will always carry out an investigation when a solicitor is convicted of a criminal offence. However, the action ultimately taken by the SRA will depend on the circumstances of the case. Under the SRA Enforcement Strategy, factors such as an inherently serious offence, substantial harm caused to others and vulnerability of the victim would all point to more severe sanctions being imposed.

📖 *SRA v Farrimond [2018] EWHC 321 (Admin)*

The solicitor in the case held a senior position in the Crown Prosecution Service. He was described as having been a competent and respected solicitor for 28 years. The solicitor pleaded guilty to the attempted murder of his wife. At the time of the offence the solicitor had been suffering from severe depression. The psychiatric evidence presented resulted in the criminal court finding that the solicitor's culpability had been reduced and imposing a reduced custodial sentence.

Nevertheless, the court dealing with the professional conduct consequences held that the only appropriate sanction was for the solicitor to be struck off. Mr Justice Garnham said: 'In my view, the commission of an offence of attempted murder, on facts such as these, is wholly incompatible with remaining on the Roll of Solicitors or remaining an officer of the Court.'

All solicitors are concerned with the administration of justice, but this Principle will be of particular significance in relation to the conduct of litigation and the duties owed by a solicitor to the court. For example, a solicitor who, in presenting the client's case, misleads the court will be in breach of Principle 1. The Principle applies, however, not only in relation to the court but also to clients and to third parties with whom the solicitor may deal.

2.4 Public trust

Principle 2 requires a solicitor to act in a way that upholds public trust and confidence in the solicitors' profession and in legal services provided by authorised persons.

It is essential for the public to be able to place trust and confidence in solicitors. In *Bolton v Law Society* [1994] 1 WLR 512 Sir Thomas Bingham MR said, 'A profession's most valuable asset is its collective reputation and the confidence which that inspires.' The reasons for this are obvious. Clients will often hand over money or assets to the safekeeping of their solicitor or disclose information which is personal in nature or commercially sensitive. Clients often instruct a solicitor when they are at their most vulnerable; for example, after suffering personal injury or following a death in the family. At all times clients are entitled to assume that their solicitor will behave professionally and protect their interests.

Understandably, the protection of the reputation of the profession in the eyes of the general public is a key aspect of the SRA's role. The actions of an individual can damage the reputation of the profession as a whole. The SRA have been at pains to point out that, for example, solicitors involved in fraudulent investment schemes have been disciplined as much for their failure to uphold public confidence in the profession as for their dishonesty.

A solicitor may harm the public's trust in the profession by behaviour outside the solicitor's practice. For example, conviction of a criminal offence wholly unconnected with the solicitor's practice would lead the solicitor to breach Principle 2.

The behaviour of the solicitor does not need to be criminal in nature in order to fall foul of Principle 2. The sending of offensive communications has been a cause for concern in recent years and has resulted in the SRA issuing specific guidance on the topic in the form of a warning notice. So, for example, sending derogatory emails to the opponent's solicitor and making offensive social media posts in a personal capacity are both examples of acts by a solicitor likely to breach Principle 2 (see **9.5.4**).

2.5 Independence

Principle 3 requires a solicitor to act with independence.

'Independence' in this context means a solicitor's own and the firm's independence, and not merely the solicitor's ability to give independent advice to a client. A solicitor should, therefore, avoid situations which might put their independence at risk, for example giving control of their practice to a third party which is beyond the regulatory reach of the SRA or other approved regulator.

✪ *Example*

Michael is a solicitor specialising in litigation. Michael is asked to act for Mr Smith, who wishes to sue Green Ltd for a substantial amount of money. The case, if successful, would also generate bad publicity for Green Ltd. Michael holds a significant number of shares in Green Ltd.

Should Michael act for Mr Smith?

Michael must ensure that his independence is not compromised. If the case is successful, this may well lead to a substantial reduction in the share price of Green Ltd, and Michael would stand to lose out financially in respect of his shares.

In these circumstances Michael could not provide unbiased and objective advice. Michael cannot act with independence and so he must therefore decline to act.

Independence includes independence from the client: 'A solicitor is independent from his client and having regard to his wider responsibilities and the need to maintain the profession's reputation, he must and should on occasion be prepared to say to his client, what you seek to do may be legal, but I am not prepared to help you to do it' (*In the matter of Paul Francis Simms*, Solicitors Disciplinary Tribunal, 2002).

2.6 Honesty

Principle 4 requires a solicitor to act with honesty.

This is one of the most fundamental principles underpinning the solicitors' profession. It is therefore not surprising that this Principle (along with Principle 5) has been singled out in the SQE1 Assessment Specification:

Candidates are required to demonstrate their ability to act **honestly** and with integrity.

It is clear from its Enforcement Strategy that the SRA considers a breach of Principle 4 to be a very serious matter:

Conduct or behaviour which demonstrates a lack of honesty or integrity are at the highest end of the spectrum, in a 'profession whose reputation depends on trust.' ...
The most serious involves proven dishonesty.

A finding of dishonesty against a solicitor will almost invariably result in the solicitor being subject to the most severe disciplinary action, namely being struck off the roll. Such sanctions may be needed to protect members of the public from any repeat of the dishonest behaviour, but will always be justified by the need to preserve the good reputation of the profession. In *Bolton v Law Society* (above) Sir Thomas Bingham MR referred to 'the need to maintain among members of the public a well-founded confidence that any solicitor whom they instruct will be a person of unquestionable integrity, probity and trustworthiness'.

The Principle is applicable not only to a solicitor's professional practice but also to life outside practice. For example, a solicitor convicted of theft will be in breach of Principle 4 and likely to be struck off even though the act of theft is completely unconnected with the solicitor's professional life.

There is an obvious overlap with the criminal law in that a solicitor convicted of a criminal offence involving dishonesty will, by definition, be in breach of Principle 4. However, a finding of dishonesty in professional conduct terms is not dependent on a conviction, or even on the solicitor's behaviour having been criminal in nature.

🔵 *Bultitude v Law Society [2004] EWCA Civ 1853*

The firm's reporting accountant declined to sign the accountant's report on the firm's accounts unless a number of old credit balances on various client ledger accounts were removed. In response, the solicitor signed a cheque transferring a composite sum of client balances to the firm's business bank account. The solicitor said that he would have returned the money to the individual clients if it had subsequently been found that the firm was not entitled to the money. The solicitor argued that he was not dishonest because he had not intended permanently to deprive anyone of anything (the requisite intention for the criminal offence of theft).

The court held that proof of dishonesty did not depend on proving an intention permanently to deprive. The solicitor had signed a cheque transferring client funds to the firm's business, without knowing or caring whether his firm was entitled to be paid those funds. That satisfied the relevant test for dishonesty. The solicitor was struck off.

In *Ivey v Genting Casinos (UK) Ltd t/a Crockfords* [2017] UKSC 67 the Supreme Court held that when dishonesty is in question, the fact-finding tribunal has first to ascertain the actual state of the individual's knowledge or belief as to the facts. The question whether the conduct was honest or dishonest must then be determined by applying the objective standards of ordinary decent people. Consequently, in determining whether a solicitor's conduct is dishonest, the SRA adopts a two-stage test:

(1) What was the solicitor's genuine knowledge or belief as to the facts at the time?

There is no requirement for the belief to have been objectively reasonable. However, reasonableness or how other solicitors may have acted can be an indicator of whether the belief was genuine.

(2) In view of the solicitor's knowledge or belief at the time, was their conduct dishonest by the standards of ordinary decent people?

This is an objective test. There is no requirement that the solicitor knew or understood that their behaviour was dishonest.

It is clear that a wide variety of acts or behaviour may be considered dishonest and therefore in breach of Principle 4. The SRA has provided the following non-exhaustive list of examples:

- taking or using someone else's money without their knowledge or agreement,
- lying to, or misleading someone, such as telling a client that their case is going well when it has failed,
- knowingly bringing a false case to a court,
- helping other people to act improperly, such as by giving credibility to a dubious or suspicious investment scheme run by others,
- giving false information to the firm's insurer,

- misleading a court, tribunal, or regulator,

- lying on a CV and misleading partners in the firm,

- backdating or creating false documents.

2.7 Integrity

Principle 5 requires a solicitor to act with integrity.

Along with Principle 4, this Principle has been singled out in the SQE1 Assessment Specification:

Candidates are required to demonstrate their ability to act honestly and with **integrity**.

This Principle will apply to all professional dealings with clients, the court, other lawyers and the public. A solicitor is in a position of trust, and so must behave in an appropriate manner to reflect that position.

There is obviously an overlap with Principle 4 in that a solicitor acting dishonestly can also be said to be acting without integrity. However, they are two distinct concepts. Integrity is wider in scope than dishonesty. This means that it is possible for a solicitor to lack integrity without being dishonest.

Wingate and another v SRA *and* Malins v SRA [2018] EWCA Civ 366

These two separate cases were heard together.

In Wingate *the solicitor was involved in obtaining a loan for the express purpose of funding litigation. In fact, the loan was used, inter alia, to repay the firm's debts. Ultimately the firm could not repay the loan in full. It was accepted that the solicitor had not acted dishonestly, but was found to have acted without integrity.*

In Malin *the solicitor had created and backdated a false letter in order to be able to recover an insurance fee under a costs order. The solicitor was found to have acted dishonestly.*

In reaching its decision, the Court of Appeal had to consider the distinction between honesty and integrity. According to Lord Justice Jackson:

Integrity is a broader concept than honesty. In professional codes of conduct the term 'integrity' is a useful shorthand to express the higher standards which society expects from professional persons and which the professions expect from their own members.

Integrity connotes adherence to the ethical standards of one's own profession. That involves more than mere honesty. To take one example, a solicitor conducting negotiations or a barrister making submissions to a judge or arbitrator will take particular care not to mislead. Such a professional person is expected to be even more scrupulous about accuracy than a member of the public in daily discourse.

The SRA approaches allegations of a lack of integrity on a case-by-case basis, taking account of the individual facts. That said, there is a wide variety of circumstances in which a solicitor could be said to have acted without integrity. The SRA has provided the following non-exhaustive list of examples of situations in which it is likely to take disciplinary action for lack of integrity:

- displaying a wilful or reckless disregard of standards, rules, legal requirements and obligations or ethics,

- taking unfair advantage of clients or third parties,

- knowingly or recklessly causing harm or distress to another,

- misleading clients or third parties.

In *Ryan Beckwith v SRA* [2020] EWHC 3231 (Admin), the court confirmed that Principle 5 is applicable to a solicitor's private life where the conduct touches realistically on the individual's practice of the profession and in a way that is demonstrably relevant. Following on from the case, the SRA has said that the closer the behaviour is to the solicitor's professional activities, workplace or relationships, and/or the more it reflects how the solicitor might behave in a professional context, the more seriously it will be regarded by the SRA. Examples of behaviour outside practice which could result in disciplinary action for a lack of integrity include sexual misconduct, bullying and making offensive/discriminatory remarks on social media in a personal capacity.

2.8 Equality, diversity and inclusion

Principle 6 requires a solicitor to act in a way that encourages equality, diversity and inclusion.

Solicitors are obviously subject to the general law. Solicitors must therefore comply with all anti-discrimination legislation, including the Equality Act 2010. Should a firm refuse to act for a client on the basis of ethnicity or sexual orientation, or fail to make reasonable adjustments to enable disabled clients to access its offices, this would amount to unlawful discrimination.

Solicitors are also under a wider duty not to discriminate in their professional dealings. Paragraph 1.1 provides that a solicitor must not unfairly discriminate by allowing their personal views to affect their professional relationships and the way in which they provide services. A finding of unlawful discrimination could also amount to a breach of Principles 1 and 2.

However, Principle 6 goes beyond a direction not to discriminate. It places a positive requirement on the solicitor to ensure that their actions encourage equality, diversity and inclusion. These are wide and distinct concepts. In very simple terms:

Equality – treating people fairly ensuring equal opportunities and not discriminating because of an individual's characteristics;

Diversity – encouraging and valuing people with a broad range of different backgrounds, knowledge, skills and experiences; understanding and respecting these individual differences;

Inclusion – acceptance and encouraging everyone to participate and contribute.

These concepts obviously impact on law firms. A firm must ensure that its recruitment process, advertising, HR policies etc encourage equality, diversity and inclusion. Additionally, the SRA expects firms to treat their employees fairly, create an inclusive workplace environment and have systems and procedures in place to address issues such as bullying, harassment, discrimination and victimisation (SRA Guidance – Workplace environment: risks of failing to protect and support colleagues).

Principle 6 is applicable to the conduct of the individual solicitor. Solicitors come into contact with a variety of people during their working day: clients, judiciary, work colleagues, counsel, expert witnesses etc. Treating those people fairly, with dignity and respect, is part and parcel of upholding the reputation of the profession. The Principle also extends to a solicitor's conduct outside practice. For example, a solicitor who, in a personal capacity, expresses racist views on social media is likely to fall foul of Principle 6.

2.9 Best interests of the client

Principle 7 requires a solicitor to act in the best interest of each client.

This Principle derives from the common law in that it reflects the fact that a solicitor is said to be in a fiduciary position in relation to a client (see **4.4.2**).

Ensuring that clients are provided with a proper standard of service in terms of client care, competence and standard of work is also encompassed by this Principle. For example, if a client is seeking advice on a subject which is beyond the solicitor's area of expertise, the solicitor would be unable to act in the best interests of the client. The best interests of the client would require the solicitor to refer the client to an expert (ideally this would be a colleague, or alternatively someone in another firm) in the relevant field of law. Equally, a solicitor must consider their capacity (in terms of work volume) to take on a particular matter. If a solicitor were to take on work when they did not have the capacity to deal with it effectively, the solicitor would be unlikely to be able to provide a proper service to that client and so would not be acting in the client's best interests.

⭐ *Example*

Yasmin is a sole practitioner who specialises in commercial property work. Yasmin is considered an expert in her field. However, Yasmin is already overworked and is struggling to keep up with her existing caseload.

Yasmin is approached by a large company. The company wants Yasmin to act on its behalf in the purchase of its new head office premises. Yasmin thinks that this work would be very lucrative for her firm.

Should Yasmin take on this work?

Yasmin must act in the best interests of her client (Principle 7), which includes providing a proper standard of service. Yasmin's expertise is not in question. However, it would appear that she does not have the capacity to take on the work. Therefore, Yasmin should decline to act, even though she would lose out on this lucrative work.

Summary

- The starting point for consideration of the Codes of Conduct and the other regulatory requirements is the seven Principles.
- The Principles set out the fundamental requirements which all individuals and firms regulated by the SRA must satisfy.
- Breach of the Principles may constitute professional misconduct.

Sample questions

Question 1

A solicitor's husband is caught by a speed camera travelling in his car at 100 mph on a 40 mph road. The husband already has several points on his driving licence and so, to avoid the husband being disqualified from driving, the solicitor makes a false statement to the police stating that she was driving the car at the time of the speeding offence.

The solicitor has been qualified for six months and works in her firm's commercial property department.

Which of the following statements best describes the professional conduct sanctions that the solicitor is likely to face?

A   The solicitor will face mild sanctions in view of her junior status.

B   The solicitor will face no sanctions because the SRA Principles do not apply to a solicitor's private life.

C   The solicitor will face mild sanctions because speeding is a minor offence.

D   The solicitor will face mild sanctions for failing to uphold public trust and confidence in the solicitors' profession.

E   The solicitor will face severe sanctions for acting dishonestly.

Answer

Option E is correct. The SRA Principles apply both inside and outside practice. The conduct issue here is the making of the false statement. In making a false statement the solicitor has acted dishonestly. Dishonesty is always regarded as serious and will attract severe sanctions. The solicitor's junior status is a relevant factor, but is unlikely to result in mild sanctions given such a deliberate and flagrant breach of Principle 4 (and Principles 2 and 5 and, arguably, Principle 1 by making a false statement to the police).

Question 2

A solicitor is instructed by a client in relation to a commercial contract. The solicitor attends a meeting with the other party's solicitor to negotiate the terms of the contract. Later that day, the solicitor tells the client that they will immediately produce a written note of what was said at the meeting. The solicitor fails to make the written note.

Some months later, a disagreement arises over the implementation of one of the terms of the contract and the client believes that having sight of exactly what was said at the meeting will resolve the disagreement. The client contacts the solicitor asking for the written note.

The solicitor cannot recall the meeting in detail, but types up a note of what the solicitor thought must have been discussed and presents it to the client, dated with the date of the meeting.

Has the solicitor acted in accordance with the SRA Principles?

A   Yes, because the solicitor has acted honestly in taking the best course of action that they could in the circumstances.

B   Yes, because the solicitor's duty to act in the best interests of the client outweighs all other considerations.

C   Yes, because the solicitor's actions have saved their firm from professional embarrassment.

D   No, because the solicitor has not acted with integrity.

E   No, because the solicitor has not acted with independence.

Answer

Option D is correct. In producing a backdated note and presenting it to the client as if it were an accurate record made a year earlier, the client has not acted with integrity (the solicitor has probably additionally breached Principle 2 and Principle 4). The solicitor's independence is not an issue of the facts (option E is therefore wrong). Producing a note which may well be inaccurate is unlikely to be in the client's best interests and in any event, Principle 7 does not outweigh all other considerations (option B is therefore wrong). Option C is wrong because acting simply in order to avoid professional embarrassment would not be complying with the Principles.

Question 3

A client instructs a solicitor to carry out the conveyancing work on the sale of a house. The client has put the house on the market for an asking price of £500,000. The solicitor thinks that the asking price is cheap. The solicitor suggests to his wife that she should buy the house. The solicitor's wife buys the property for £500,000 and sells it three months later, making a profit of £75,000.

Which of the following best describes the professional conduct implications of the solicitor's actions?

A   The solicitor did not do anything wrong because the client achieved their objective of selling the house.

B   The solicitor's actions are likely to diminish public trust and confidence in the solicitors' profession because a profit has been made at the client's expense.

C   The solicitor did not do anything wrong because the client did not suffer a loss.

D   The solicitor acted with integrity because the solicitor did not make a profit himself.

E   The solicitor acted in the client's best interests in securing the price the client wanted for the house.

Answer

Option B is correct. The solicitor placed his own interests and those of his family above those of a client. The solicitor's wife has made a profit at the client's expense. Such behaviour is likely to diminish public trust and confidence in the profession and therefore breach Principle 2. The solicitor has not acted with integrity in making a profit for his family and so has breached Principle 5 (accordingly, option D is wrong). The client has achieved the objective of selling the house, but the solicitor did not act correctly (option A is wrong). The solicitor is in breach of Principle 2 irrespective of the fact that the client has not suffered a loss and was paid the asking price (accordingly, options C and E are wrong).

3 Obtaining Instructions

SQE1 syllabus

This chapter will help you to achieve the SQE1 Assessment Specification in relation to Functioning Legal Knowledge concerned with Ethics and Professional Conduct on:

- the purpose, scope and content of the SRA Principles,

- the purpose, scope and content of the SRA Code of Conduct for Solicitors, RELs and RFLs.

Ethics and Professional Conduct is a pervasive topic in SQE1 and may be examined across all subject areas.

Note that for SQE1, candidates are not usually required to recall specific case names or cite statutory or regulatory authorities. Cases are provided for illustrative purposes only.

Learning outcomes

By the end of this chapter you will be able to demonstrate your ability to act honestly and with integrity, and in accordance with the SRA Standards and Regulations in relation to:

- client information and publicity; and

- referrals, introductions and separate businesses.

3.1 Introduction

A solicitors' firm is a business, and has much in common with, say, a high street store or goods manufacturer. Obviously, a firm of solicitors sells services rather than goods but, just like other businesses, it needs a regular supply of customers to survive. Without clients, a solicitors' firm cannot generate income to pay staff salaries, the rent on premises or for the upkeep of the office equipment. Accordingly, just like other businesses, a firm of solicitors must take steps to try to maintain and increase its market share. The two most common ways of trying to achieve this are through advertising and referrals.

This chapter looks at:

- general principles
- advertising
- referrals
- arrangements with third parties
- referral fees
- separate businesses.

3.2 General principles

Solicitors have always sought to secure more work; however, historically, the steps which firms could take to attract new clients were severely restricted. Nowadays there are fewer restrictions. Marketing has become an increasingly important function within firms with individual solicitors being expected to play their part in promoting the firm and its services.

A firm must take steps to try to maintain and increase its market share in order to prosper as a business. However, no matter how urgent these financial pressures may be, a solicitor must at all times comply with the requirements of professional conduct, and in particular with the SRA Principles. Of particular relevance in this context will be maintaining independence (Principle 3) and acting in the client's best interests (Principle 7).

In seeking to attract new work or otherwise increase the firm's income, a solicitor must not do anything or enter into any arrangement that would compromise the solicitor's independence or restrict the solicitor from acting in the best interests of the client. For example, a firm may be offered a large financial incentive to refer all clients requiring advice on financial services to a particular firm of brokers. However, the firm must not accept this offer if it would prevent solicitors acting in the best interests of their clients.

3.3 Advertising

3.3.1 The need for advertising

In the past, it was common for solicitors to rely on their personal reputation to obtain work. For example, a solicitor would earn a reputation for a certain type of work (eg family law) by word of mouth in a town or city. This method of obtaining work is still valuable today. One of the best ways of attracting clients is by personal recommendation of a friend or colleague who has experienced similar problems. There are also publications, such as the Legal 500, which list the names of the 'top' solicitors in a particular legal field and geographical location.

However, in recent times firms have invested substantial sums of money with a view to attracting new clients through different means. For example, firms will advertise their services in local newspapers, on their websites or through promotional literature. The use of radio and television advertisements has become more frequent in recent years (particularly in the area of personal injury work). Social media has also been embraced by the profession in order to engage with current and potential clients and to market its services.

The aim of these advertisements is to increase the general public's awareness of the firm in question, and of the services that the firm offers (ie how the firm could help the potential client). Therefore, when a potential client needs the services of a solicitor, they will know which firm to contact.

Solicitors are generally free to publicise their practice provided they comply with both the general law and the requirements of professional conduct.

3.3.2 General law

By the very nature of their work solicitors hold a good deal of information about their client's and others. Such information must not be misused. The UK General Data Protection Regulation (GDPR) and the Data Protection Act 2018 (DPA 2018) require those who are 'controllers' or 'processors' of personal information to handle it in particular ways, and impose penalties on processors who are in breach of their duties. The precise details of the duties and penalties are beyond the scope of this manual, but, broadly, personal information is defined in the GDPR as 'any information relating to an identified or identifiable natural person', controlling means determining the purpose and manner in which personal data is processed, and processing includes collecting, recording, organising, storing and disclosing such information, whether by automated or manual methods.

A data processor must comply with all six principles set out in the GDPR (eg personal data must be accurate and, where necessary, kept up to date), and a data controller is responsible for, and must be able to demonstrate compliance with, these principles. A data controller can only process data on one or more of the six legal grounds in the GDPR or a public interest ground set out in the DPA 1998. A data processor may have to obtain express consent from a person about whom data is collected and stored ('a data subject'), and the data subject will have rights over their data, including the right to see the data by making a subject access request and to have the data erased in certain circumstances, for example where personal data is no longer necessary for their intended collection and processing purpose.

There are various other legislative provisions on advertising and data protection including the UK Code of Non-broadcast Advertising and Direct and Promotional Marketing (CAP Code).

3.3.3 Professional conduct requirements

3.3.3.1 General provisions

The SRA considers that there is an imbalance of knowledge between the general public on the one hand and the solicitor providing the service on the other. Accordingly, publicity in relation to the firm must be accurate and not misleading, including that relating to charges and the circumstances in which interest is payable by or to clients (Paragraph 8.8). This also applies to marketing material used by a third party that the solicitor may work with (see **3.4**).

The term 'publicity' is very widely defined and includes all promotional material and activity, including the name and description of the firm, stationery, advertisements, brochures, websites, directory entries, media appearances, promotional press releases and direct approaches to potential clients and other persons, whether conducted in person, in writing or electronic form (SRA Glossary). It does not, however, include press releases prepared on behalf of a client.

3.3.3.2 SRA Transparency Rules

The stated aim of the SRA Transparency Rules is to ensure that consumers of legal services have accurate and relevant information about a solicitor or firm when they are considering purchasing legal services. Such information should help consumers to make informed choices and improve competition in the legal market. The Rules require all firms regulated by the SRA (and individual freelance solicitors and solicitors providing services to the public from outside SRA-authorised firms), who publish as part of their usual business the availability of any of the services specified in the Rules, to publish certain information about the costs of those services. This does not apply to publicly funded work. The Rules set the minimum information that must be provided. However, the SRA encourages firms to provide additional information if it would be helpful for consumers.

The specified services in relation to individuals are:

- residential conveyancing,

- uncontested probate (where all assets are within the UK),

- motoring offences (summary only offences),

- employment tribunals (claims for unfair or wrongful dismissal),

- immigration (excluding asylum applications).

The specified services in relation to businesses are:

- debt recovery (up to £100,000),

- employment tribunals (defending claims for unfair or wrongful dismissal),

- licensing applications for business premises.

The information on the costs must include the following:

(a) the total cost of the service or, where this is not practicable, the average cost or range of costs, and details of any disbursements;

(b) the basis for the charges (including any hourly rate or fixed fees);

(c) what services are included within the displayed price and details of any services which might reasonably be expected to be included in the price but are not;

(d) the experience and qualifications of anyone carrying out the work (and their supervisors);

(e) whether VAT is payable on the fees or disbursements and, if so, if this is included in the price;

(f) typical timescales and the key stages of the matter;

(g) if conditional fee or damages-based agreements are used, the circumstances in which clients may have to make any payments themselves for the services received (including from any damages).

The costs information must be published in a prominent place on the website which is accessible, clearly signposted and easy to find. Where the firm or solicitor does not have a website, the Rules require that the information must be made available on request.

3.3.3.3 Unsolicited approaches

A solicitor may wish to 'cold call' individuals in order to promote the solicitor's business. A solicitor must comply with the general law applicable to such marketing. This means that the solicitor must have all consents required by the relevant data protection legislation for the type of marketing the solicitor intends to carry out.

Data protection legislation also permits all individuals to request that their details are not used for direct marketing purposes, and therefore if a solicitor receives such a request, it should be taken seriously and complied with.

In addition, Paragraph 8.9 prohibits a solicitor from making unsolicited approaches to individual members of the public which, even if permitted by law, may feel unwelcome or intrusive. However, there is an exception in respect of current or former clients in order to advertise legal services provided by the firm or solicitor. Unsolicited approaches made to current or potential business contacts would not count as being made 'to members of the public' for these purposes and so are permitted provided they comply with the general law.

Paragraph 8.9 is intended to prevent direct or specifically targeted approaches to members of the public in person, by phone or other means. Newspaper and TV advertisements are in a sense 'unsolicited' approaches, but would not be caught by Paragraph 8.9 because they are not individual or targeted and so could not be regarded as intrusive.

In its Guidance: Unsolicited approaches (advertising) to members of the public, the SRA draws a distinction between sending leaflets to all homes in a large geographic area and selectively distributing leaflets to only specific homes or individuals based on wider information. The former is permitted because it would not be a targeted approach.

✪ Example

Misbah is a solicitor. Misbah's firm expects all its fee earners to play an active role in promoting the success of the business. The firm is conducting a marketing drive. The firm's marketing department has identified a number of former clients who have not used the firm for a number of years. The marketing department suggests that a representative from the firm telephones these former clients to try to convince them to use the firm again.

The marketing department also suggests a campaign of door-to-door visits on a nearby new luxury housing development where a representative of the firm would tell the home owners about the services provided by the firm's private client and property teams and take their contact details for a follow-up email.

Should Misbah agree to take part in these marketing activities?

Whilst a solicitor must not make unsolicited telephone calls to members of the public, the solicitor may do so to current and former clients (Paragraph 8.9). Misbah can cold call former clients so long as he complies with the provisions of the data protection legislation and the general law. However, the proposed campaign of door-to-door visits would amount to unsolicited approaches to members of the public. Personal visits are likely to be considered as intrusive and the campaign appears targeted at wealthy individuals in a small area. Misbah should not undertake door-to-door visits.

3.3.3.4 Letterheads, websites and emails

A solicitor must not be a manager, employee, member or interest holder of a business that has a name which includes the word 'solicitors' or describes its work in a way that suggests that it is a solicitors' firm unless it is a body authorised by the SRA (Paragraph 5.4).

Likewise, there is an obligation to ensure that clients understand whether and how the services provided are regulated, including explaining which activities will be carried out as a person authorised by the SRA, any services which may be regulated by another approved regulator and ensuring that no business or employer is represented as being regulated by the SRA when it is not (Paragraph 8.10).

The Transparency Rules require that a body authorised by the SRA must display in a prominent place on its website its SRA number and the SRA's 'digital badge' (a 'clickable' logo which confirms that it is regulated and links to information on the protections this offers its clients). The website must publish the firm's complaints handling process, together with details about how to complain to the SRA and the Legal Ombudsman. In addition, its letterhead and emails must show its SRA authorisation number and the words 'authorised and regulated by the Solicitors Regulations Authority'.

3.3.3.5 Social media

Whilst there are no specific provisions in the Code of Conduct that apply to the use of social media by solicitors, regard must still be had to the Principles and the relevant standards in the Code when using social media as a marketing tool. For example, if a relationship with a client is established and continued via social media, the solicitor must still comply with the standards in the Code of Conduct on service and competence (see **Chapter 5**) and with regard to confidentiality and disclosure (see **Chapter 6**).

A Law Society practice note on social media notes the commercial benefits, but also highlights the potential risks, especially as it continues to evolve with the integration of artificial intelligence. For example, a solicitor posting on social media that they are in a certain location at a certain time may unintentionally disclose that they are working with a client and thereby breach client confidentiality (see **Chapter 6**). The practice note offers a salutary warning: 'One misplaced comment, opinion, or a "like" from a legal professional may not only damage that individual's reputation, and their fitness or propriety as a regulated individual, but could reflect negatively on the legal profession more generally.'

3.4 Arrangements with third parties

In addition to targeting the general public, a solicitor may also wish to enter into an agreement with a third party to introduce clients to the solicitor. For example, a solicitor could enter into an agreement with a local estate agent, so that the agent will 'introduce' to the solicitor's firm any potential house buyers looking for a solicitor to complete their conveyancing, or with a claims management company to 'introduce' clients who wish to claim for losses arising from a motor vehicle accident. Likewise, the solicitor may want to enter into an agreement to refer clients to a third party, such as another lawyer or a financial services provider. Any such arrangement must comply with the SRA Principles and the relevant paragraphs of the Code of Conduct for Solicitors.

As the relationship between a solicitor and the client should be built on trust, it follows that any arrangement with a third party should not jeopardise that trust and that a solicitor must not abuse their position by taking unfair advantage of clients or others (Paragraph 1.2).

A solicitor may refer a client to a third party. In respect of such a referral the client must be informed of any financial or other interest which the solicitor, the solicitor's business or employer has in referring the client to another person/body (Paragraph 5.1(a)).

A client may be introduced to the solicitor by a third party. The term 'introducer' is defined in the SRA Glossary as 'any person, business or organisation who or that introduces or refers clients to your business, or recommends your business to clients or otherwise puts you and clients in touch with one another'. Any client referred to the solicitor by an introducer must not have been acquired in a way which would breach the SRA's regulatory arrangements if the person acquiring the client were regulated by the SRA (Paragraph 5.1(e)). So, for example, the client must not have been acquired as a result of 'cold calling'. The SRA Warning Notice, 'Marketing your services to members of the public', says that the solicitor must be able to demonstrate that the third party did not acquire the client through prohibited means and must make sure that the third party is aware of the solicitor's regulatory duties and how these impact on the way that the third party works. The client must be informed of any financial or other interest which the introducer has in introducing the client to the solicitor (Paragraph 5.1(a)).

A solicitor must not receive payments relating to a referral or make payment to an introducer in respect of clients who are the subject of criminal proceedings (para 5.1(d)).

Fee-sharing would occur if a solicitor made a payment to a third party in respect of a percentage of the solicitor's gross or net fees for a particular period. Clients must be informed of any fee-sharing arrangement that is relevant to their matter, and the fee-sharing agreement must be in writing (Paragraph 5.1(b) and (c)).

⭐ *Example*

> *Peri is a solicitor. Peri is contacted by Monks and Co., a well-established local firm of independent financial advisers. Monks and Co. proposes entering into an agreement whereby Peri refers to it all of her clients seeking advice about insurance products. In return, Monks and Co. will pay Peri a small commission for each client referred.*
>
> *Can Peri accept this proposition?*
>
> *Peri would be able to enter into such an agreement so long as she is satisfied that in referring clients to Monks and Co. she is acting with independence (Principle 3), so that, for example, Peri did not feel that her freedom to refer clients to other providers of financial advice is then restricted. In making the referrals, Peri must also be acting in the best interests of each client (Principle 7). Clients must be informed of the commission arrangement with Monks and Co. (para 5.1(a)). (Peri would also need to account properly to the client for any financial benefit (the commission) she receives as a result of that client's instructions (para 4.1) (see **Chapter 5**).)*

3.5 'Referral fees'

Historically there was a ban on solicitors paying or receiving referral fees. Although the blanket ban was lifted in 2004, referral fees are still prohibited by legislation in certain circumstances. Under the Legal Aid, Sentencing and Punishment of Offenders Act 2012 (LASPO), the payment or receipt of referral fees in claims for damages following personal injury or death is prohibited. LASPO also prohibits payment for other claims for damages arising from the same circumstances. For example, if a personal injury claim resulting from a road traffic accident is referred to a solicitor, together with a claim in relation to uninsured loss recovery resulting from the same accident, the solicitor could not pay a referral fee in relation to either claim.

Under Paragraph 5.2, where it appears to the SRA that a solicitor has made or received a 'referral fee', the payment will be treated as such a fee unless the solicitor is able to show otherwise. The term 'referral fee' in this context is defined in the SRA Glossary by reference to the relevant provisions of LASPO and so, as outlined above, refers to prohibited fees in personal injury cases.

3.6 Separate businesses

A separate business essentially means a business which is owned by or connected with a body authorised by the SRA, or which owns the authorised body or in which the authorised body directly participates in the provision of its services and which is not itself authorised by the SRA or another approved regulator or an overseas practice (SRA Glossary). The SRA considers it important that the public is not confused or misled by a solicitor or firm incorporating non-regulated services into their practice, not least because the protection (if any) they obtain in using such services can be different from that for mainstream legal services regulated by the SRA.

Solicitors should ensure that they do not represent any separate business as being regulated by the SRA (Paragraph 8.10(c)). Historically, examples of the kinds of services that a separate business offered are alternative dispute resolution, financial services and an estate agency. However, the SRA Authorisation of Firms Rules permit recognised bodies and sole practices to offer a wider range of services than before, including the kind of services mentioned above, and so a separate business would no longer be required in order to offer these.

A solicitor can only refer, recommend or introduce a client to the separate business or divide, or allow to be divided, a client's matter between their regulated business and the separate business where the client has given informed consent (Paragraph 5.3).

Summary

- Solicitors should always be independent when giving advice to a client and ensure that their clients' interests are protected.

- Solicitors are free to publicise their practice, provided that they comply with the general law on advertising in force at the time and with the relevant standards of the Codes of Conduct.

- A solicitor's promotional material must not be misleading or inaccurate.

- Solicitors may enter into a financial arrangement with an introducer, refer clients to third parties and enter into fee-sharing arrangements, provided that they comply with Paragraphs 5.1 and 5.2.

Sample questions

Question 1

A solicitor is invited by the manager of a local care home to give an informative talk to the home's elderly residents on the importance of making a will. The solicitor gives the talk to those residents who have expressed an interest in the subject matter and, in doing so, presents an even-handed and accurate explanation of the advantages and disadvantages of making a will. At the end of the talk the solicitor hands out leaflets advertising the solicitor's firm's will drafting services. The solicitor also offers to draw up a will there and then for any residents that would like the solicitor to do so.

Which of the following best describes the consequences of the solicitor's actions under the SRA Code of Conduct for Solicitors, RELS and RFLs?

A   All of the solicitor's actions breach the Code because they are unsolicited approaches to members of the public.

B   The solicitor is unlikely to have done anything wrong in giving the talk, but handing out the leaflets and offering to draw up wills breach the Code as unsolicited approaches to members of the public.

C   The solicitor is unlikely to have done anything wrong in giving the talk and handing out the leaflets, but offering to draw up wills breaches the Code as an unsolicited approach to members of the public.

D   None of the solicitor's actions breach the Code because making a will is in the client's best interests.

E   None of the solicitor's actions breach the Code because the solicitor has acted in response to the manager's invitation and so the solicitor's approaches are not unsolicited.

Answer

Option B is correct. Giving an informative and even-handed talk to an interested audience is unlikely to breach the Code (option A is therefore wrong). But in going beyond this the solicitor is publicising services through a targeted and intrusive approaches to members of the public, and consequently is in breach of Paragraph 8.9 (the solicitor may also be criticised for taking advantage of a vulnerable client (see **4.4.3**)). Option E is wrong; the approaches are unsolicited by the ultimate clients and so the manager's invitation is irrelevant. Option D is wrong; it may be a good idea for the client to make a will, but this does not absolve the solicitor of their obligations under Paragraph 8.9.

Question 2

A solicitor has been acting in a divorce case for a successful local businessman. The divorce case is now at an end. The firm's senior partner tells the solicitor to telephone the businessman in order to promote the firm's corporate department in the hope that the businessman will transfer the corporate work arising from his various business interests from his current lawyers to the solicitor's firm.

Which of the following best explains what the solicitor should do?

A   Make the telephone call because any breach of the SRA Code of Conduct for Solicitors, RELs and RFLs will be the senior partner's responsibility.

B   Make the telephone call because such a call would not constitute an unsolicited approach to a member of the public.

C   Refuse to make the telephone call because such a call would constitute advertising.

D   Refuse to make the telephone call because the solicitor no longer acts for the client.

E   Refuse to make the telephone call because the solicitor could not make such a call and comply with their duty to act with integrity.

Answer

Option B is correct. Paragraph 8.9 prohibits a solicitor making unsolicited approaches to members of the public. However, a former client is an exception (accordingly, option D is wrong). There is nothing inherent in the making of the call which would place the solicitor in breach of the duty to act with integrity (option C is wrong). Solicitors are able to advertise. Option A is wrong – a solicitor is personally accountable for compliance with the SRA Code of Conduct for Solicitors, RELs and RFLs.

Question 3

An estate agent is undertaking a marketing campaign trying to acquire new clients by making targeted face-to-face visits to properties in the area worth over £1 million to see if the owners are willing to sell.

The estate agent contacts a solicitor and suggests that it would be mutually beneficial for the estate agent to recommend to all clients acquired from the campaign that they instruct the solicitor to do the conveyancing work for them. The estate agent suggests that in return they are paid 1% of the solicitor's conveyancing fees for each client who instructs the solicitor as a result of the recommendation.

The solicitor agrees to the estate agent's suggestion and they enter into a written agreement to that effect. The agreement provides that every client must be informed of the estate agent's financial interest in making the recommendation.

Does the agreement breach the SRA Code of Conduct for Solicitors, RELs and RFLs?

A   No, because the agreement is in writing.

B   No, because every client is informed of the estate agent's financial interest in making the recommendation.

C   No, because the solicitor is not making any direct approach to the clients.

D   Yes, because solicitors are not permitted to share their fees.

E   Yes, because the estate agent is acquiring the clients by making unsolicited approaches to members of the public.

Answer

Option E is correct. Solicitors are permitted to enter into fee-sharing arrangements of this kind (as a result option D is wrong). Such agreements must be in writing (Paragraph 5.1(c)) and clients must be informed of the introducer's financial interest (Paragraph 5.1(a)). However, the solicitor must ensure that clients are not recruited in a way which would be in breach of the Code of Conduct for Solicitors if done by the solicitor themselves (Paragraph 5.1(e)). Here the clients are being recruited by cold calling and so the solicitor is in breach of the Code of Conduct for Solicitors (Paragraph 8.9).

4 The Retainer

SQE1 syllabus

This chapter will help you to achieve the SQE1 Assessment Specification in relation to Functioning Legal Knowledge concerned with Ethics and Professional Conduct on:

- the purpose, scope and content of the SRA Principles,

- the purpose, scope and content of the SRA Code of Conduct for Solicitors, RELs and RFLs.

Ethics and Professional Conduct is a pervasive topic in SQE1 and may be examined across all subject areas.

Note that for SQE1, candidates are not usually required to recall specific case names or cite statutory or regulatory authorities. Cases are provided for illustrative purposes only.

Learning outcomes

By the end of this chapter you will be able to demonstrate your ability to act honestly and with integrity, and in accordance with the SRA Standards and Regulations in relation to:

- maintaining trust and acting fairly;

- client identification; and

- service and competence.

4.1 Introduction

The contract between a solicitor and the client is often referred to as a 'retainer'. As with any other contract, the relationship between the solicitor and the client is governed by the general law. However, in addition to considering the general law, a solicitor must also comply with obligations placed upon them by the requirements of professional conduct.

This chapter looks at:

- accepting instructions
- refusal of instructions to act
- duties to the client during the retainer
- the client's authority
- termination of the retainer
- liens.

4.2 Accepting instructions

4.2.1 Terms of the retainer

Many of the terms of the retainer will be implied into the contract either by the law, or by the requirements of professional conduct. However, the solicitor must ensure that the more basic terms of the retainer are understood by the client.

One critical issue is to ensure that the client understands exactly what work the solicitor has agreed to undertake. Although not required by the Code of Conduct for Solicitors, it would be good practice for a solicitor to send a letter to the client at the start of the transaction, confirming to the client exactly what the solicitor understands their instructions to be. This will help to avoid any misunderstandings at a later date.

It is important that a client's expectations are managed at an early stage of the solicitor–client relationship. If the client knows what the solicitor will and will not be doing for the client, there will be less scope for problems to arise.

4.2.2 Identity of the client

A solicitor must identify whom they are acting for in relation to any matter (Paragraph 8.1). For example, a solicitor may be instructed by a director of a company concerning the debts of that company. The solicitor will be obliged to clarify whether the solicitor is being instructed by the director in their personal capacity, or by the director on behalf of the company (the company will be the client, not the director personally). A solicitor owes many duties to the client, and the solicitor can only ensure that these duties are met if they know the identity of the client.

However, the primary purpose behind Paragraph 8.1 is to try to prevent solicitors inadvertently becoming involved in fraud. Solicitors are at particular risk of becoming unwittingly caught up in the actions of fraudsters. An area which has seen a significant rise in the number of cases in recent years is property and title fraud where wrongdoers have engaged in such activities as impersonating registered proprietors, creating false conveyancing firms and submitting forged documents. In such cases, solicitors may become innocent victims.

P&P Property Ltd v Owen White & Catlin LLP and Another; Dreamvar (UK) Ltd v Mishcon De Reya and Another [2018] EWCA Civ 1082

These cases were heard together as they contained similar facts.

In both cases, a fraudulent seller had purported to sell a high-value London property to an innocent buyer. In fact, the fraudsters did not own the properties, but this was not discovered until after the purchase monies had been handed over. The Court of Appeal held that, although there was no negligence on the part of the buyers' solicitors, they were liable for the losses suffered by their buyer clients. This was on the basis that the buyers' solicitors had received the money from their clients on trust to use for a genuine completion. As there had not, in fact, been a genuine completion, the buyers' solicitors were in breach of trust. This was despite the fact that, in the Mishcon De Reya case, the seller's solicitor had not carried out adequate identity checks on its own client. The Court held that the seller's solicitor was not liable in tort to the buyer or their solicitor, as it had no general duty of care to them. However, the buyer's solicitor could claim a contribution from the seller's solicitor towards the buyer's losses, as the previous edition of the Law Society's Code for Completion by Post, which the parties had adopted, required the seller's solicitor to use the purchase money for a genuine completion (as a result of the case the Code was changed and now expressly provides that the seller's solicitor holds the purchase moneys on trust for the buyer and is under a fiduciary duty not to deal with that money other than in accordance with the terms of the Code).

The outcome of these cases may seem harsh on the buyers' solicitors, as the losses stemmed from the actions of a party who was not their client, and whose identify and status they were not in a position to easily check. The cases serve as a warning of the prevalence of fraud and a reminder of the need for vigilance on the part of solicitors.

To reduce the risk of inadvertently becoming involved in fraud a solicitor must take steps to establish who they are dealing with at the outset. It is for the solicitor to decide what steps are appropriate, but the SRA suggests that a proportionate approach should be adopted, taking account of such factors as the size of the firm, the number of fee earners, the client profile, the different areas of work the firm does and the particular risks involved in those areas of work.

A solicitor is also under a separate duty to obtain 'satisfactory evidence' of the identity of their clients (ie is the client actually the person they claim to be?). This obligation is imposed by the Money Laundering, Terrorist Financing and Transfer of Funds (Information on the Payer) Regulations 2017 (SI 2017/692) (see **Legal Services**).

4.2.3 Third party instructions

A solicitor may receive instructions from a third party on behalf of a client. For example, a client's daughter may seek to instruct a solicitor on behalf of her elderly mother, as the mother may have mobility problems in attending the solicitor's office or a director may instruct a solicitor on behalf of a company.

Alternatively, a solicitor may receive instructions from one client purporting to instruct the solicitor on behalf of a number of clients. For example, a solicitor may be instructed by Mr Smith to purchase a property on behalf of Mr Smith and Mr Brown. (When considering whether to accept instructions from or on behalf of a number of clients, the solicitor must also take into account any actual or potential conflicts of interests (see **Chapter 7**).)

The Code of Conduct for Solicitors provides that a solicitor only acts for clients on instructions from the client, or from someone properly authorised to provide instructions on their behalf (Paragraph 3.1). Therefore, in the examples given above, the solicitor must satisfy themselves that the daughter has the proper authorisation to provide instructions for her mother, that the director is authorised to give instructions on behalf of the client and that Mr Smith has authority to provide instructions on a joint basis for himself and Mr Brown.

A lack of authority has further repercussions in a litigation matter. In taking any positive step in court proceedings (such as issuing proceedings) a solicitor warrants that they have authority to do so. If a solicitor conducts proceedings without that authority, the solicitor will usually be personally liable for the costs incurred.

⬛ *Warner v Masefield [2008] EWHC 1129 (Ch)*

A firm of solicitors issued proceedings on behalf of two trustees. In fact, the firm had only been instructed by one trustee and that trustee had no authority to give instructions on behalf of the other. The court held that in accepting instructions from only one trustee the firm had breached the version of the Code of Conduct then in force and that the firm was in breach of its implied authority to act. The firm was ordered to pay the costs of the other parties involved.

4.3 Refusal of instructions to act

Solicitors are keen both to attract new clients to their business and retain their existing clients. However, there will be some clients for whom a solicitor will decline to act. For example, a solicitor may decline to act for a client who is known for not paying their legal fees.

Generally, like any other business, a solicitor is free to decide whether to accept or decline instructions to act for a particular client. However, this discretion is limited by the requirements of professional conduct and also by the general law. A solicitor must not unfairly discriminate by allowing their views to affect their professional relationships and the way in which the solicitor provides services (Paragraph 1.1). A solicitor would therefore be in breach of the Code of Conduct for Solicitors if, by refusing to accept a client's instructions, it could be shown that the solicitor was unfairly discriminating against that client because of, for example, the client's race or gender.

4.3.1 Duress or undue influence and vulnerable clients

If a solicitor has reason to suspect that the instructions received from a client, or someone authorised on their behalf, do not represent the client's wishes, the solicitor must not act unless they have satisfied themselves that they do (Paragraph 3.1).

There may be situations where a solicitor has reasonable grounds for believing that the instructions are affected by duress or undue influence. The elderly, those with language or learning difficulties or those with mental health issues are particularly susceptible to undue pressure from others. In circumstances in which a solicitor suspects a client's instructions are tainted by duress or undue influence, it would be necessary for the solicitor to take appropriate steps to satisfy themselves that the instructions represent the client's genuine wishes, for example by arranging to interview the client alone, away from any third party such as a relative. If, having taken such steps, the solicitor is not satisfied, the solicitor should decline to act for that client. Alternatively, in circumstances in which the solicitor has concerns that the client is under duress, the solicitor may seek assistance from the High Court to provide its protection under its inherent jurisdiction.

In circumstances where the solicitor has legal authority to act for a client notwithstanding that it is not possible to obtain or ascertain the instructions of the client, then the solicitor is subject to the overriding obligation to protect the client's best interests (Paragraph 3.1). This would include, for example, where a solicitor has been authorised by the Court of Protection to act for a client who lacks mental capacity under the Mental Capacity Act 2005.

✪ *Example*

Oskar is a solicitor. Oskar is instructed by Alfie on behalf of his elderly mother. Alfie instructs Oskar to transfer his mother's house into Alfie's name. Alfie gives Oskar a letter purportedly from his mother confirming these instructions. Alfie explains that her age means that she is unable to visit Oskar's office to speak with him in person.

Should Oskar accept these instructions?

There are two issues here. First, as Oskar has received these instructions from a third party, he should satisfy himself that Alfie has the proper authority to give those instructions.

Second, the circumstances (the mother's age, the facts that she is gifting away a valuable asset and her absence from Oskar's office) should give reasonable grounds to suspect duress or undue influence. Oskar should therefore not act for the mother without satisfying himself that the instructions represent her wishes. To do so, Oskar would need, for example, to interview her away from her son and assess whether he believes she genuinely wishes to transfer her house to her son.

Where there is no actual evidence of undue influence but the client insists on acting in a way which appears to be to their disadvantage, it would be advisable to explain the consequences of the instructions and ask the client whether they wish to proceed, and for this advice and consent to be documented.

4.3.2 Duty to act in the client's best interests

A solicitor must act in the best interests of each client (Principle 7). Accordingly, a solicitor must not accept instructions in circumstances where the solicitor will be unable to meet this fundamental requirement. This might occur where there is an own interest conflict or a conflict of interest (see **Chapter 7**) or where the solicitor holds 'material' confidential information for an existing or former client which would be relevant to a new instruction (see **Chapter 6**).

A solicitor must ensure that the service provided to clients is competent and delivered in a timely manner and must consider and take account of the client's attributes, needs and circumstances (Paragraphs 3.2 and 3.4). Accordingly, a solicitor must consider the level and quality of service the solicitor will be able to provide to the client. If the solicitor lacks the time, resources or expertise to deal with the client's matter then it would not be in that client's best interests for the solicitor to accept the instruction.

4.3.3 Gifts from clients

There may be situations where a client proposes to make a gift of significant value to a solicitor, a member of the solicitor's family or to a member of the solicitor's firm or that person's family. Typically, the solicitor may be asked to draft a will for a client which includes a significant gift to the solicitor. The question arises, therefore, as to when it would be appropriate to accept such instructions and when it would be appropriate to advise the client to take independent legal advice.

There are no specific references in the Code of Conduct for Solicitors to this type of situation. However, the Law Society has issued a practice note which offers some guidance. It advises that a solicitor should carefully consider any gift to determine whether it may be considered significant in the particular circumstances, and that it can be assumed that it would be significant if:

(a) it is worth more than 1% of the client's current estimated net estate;

(b) it might become valuable at some point, especially after the death of the client;

(c) it provides a benefit to an individual which is more valuable than his relationship to the deceased reasonably justifies.

Drafting a will which includes a significant gift to the solicitor gives rise to the potential for an own interest conflict (Paragraph 6.1) (see **Chapter 7**). In its Guidance: Drafting and Preparation of Wills, the SRA says that usually the effect of Paragraph 6.1 will be to prevent the solicitor acting unless the solicitor is satisfied that the client has taken independent legal advice on making the gift. However, each case must be considered on its own facts. The Guidance goes on to give an example of a situation where it may be still appropriate to draft the will even if the client has not received independent legal advice. This is where the solicitor is drafting wills for the solicitor's own parents and the survivor of them wishes to leave the residuary estate to the solicitor and their siblings in equal shares.

4.3.4 Compliance with the law and the Code of Conduct

In deciding whether to act, a solicitor must act in a way that upholds the constitutional principle of the rule of law, and the proper administration of justice (Principle 1). For example, a solicitor instructed on the sale of a property might be instructed to tamper with a surveyor's report and send it to the buyer in order to hide some defects in the structure of the property. If the solicitor agreed, they would be participating in fraud against the buyer. Clearly, instructions must be refused here.

If the acceptance of the instructions would place the solicitor in breach of the Code of Conduct for Solicitors, the solicitor must refuse to act. Examples of instructions which would not comply with the Code are where:

(a) there is, or is likely to be, a conflict of interest between the solicitor and the client, or between two or more clients (see **Chapter 7**);

(b) the solicitor holds material confidential information for an existing or former client which would be relevant to a new instruction (see **Chapter 6**);

(c) the client instructs the solicitor to mislead or deceive the court (see **Chapter 9**).

A solicitor must also be able to justify their decisions and actions in order to demonstrate compliance with the solicitor's obligations under the SRA's regulatory arrangements (Paragraph 7.2).

4.4 Duties to the client during the retainer

A solicitor will owe the client a number of duties throughout the retainer. These duties are prescribed by the common law and the requirements of professional conduct. Some of these duties (such as the duty of confidentiality (see **Chapter 6**)) will continue even after the retainer has been terminated.

4.4.1 Duty of reasonable care and skill

In addition to the solicitor's duty of care in common law, s 13 Supply of Goods and Services Act 1982 provides that a supplier of services will carry out those services with reasonable care and skill. This term is implied into the retainer between a solicitor and the client, and therefore the solicitor may be sued for a breach of contract if the term is breached. However, this implied term does not apply to advocacy services provided before a court, tribunal, inquiry or arbitrator (Supply of Services (Exclusion of Implied Terms) Order 1982 (SI 1982/1771), art 2).

Nevertheless, the solicitor may be sued for negligence in both contentious and non-contentious proceedings. The House of Lords removed an advocate's protection from negligence claims in *Arthur JS Hall & Co v Simons* [2002] 1 AC 615. Accordingly, a solicitor who acts as an advocate may be sued in the tort of negligence if the solicitor breaches their duty of care to the client within court proceedings.

4.4.2 Duty to act in the client's best interests

As a matter of professional conduct, a solicitor must act in the best interests of the client (Principle 7 (see **Chapter 2**)). However, this is also a duty placed on a solicitor at common law.

The solicitor–client relationship is said to be a 'fiduciary relationship'. Under the common law, a fiduciary relationship is one where one party must act in the best interests of the other party. This means that the solicitor must put the interests of the client before their own.

Where such a relationship exists, one party may not make a secret profit at the expense of the other party. For example, a solicitor may be paid commission, say £50, when referring a client to a third party such as an accountant. As the solicitor owes a fiduciary duty to the client, this £50 must be accounted for to the client. This duty to account is also mirrored by Paragraph 4.1. A solicitor is also under more general obligations to safeguard money and assets entrusted to the solicitor by clients (and others) (Paragraph 4.2) and not to hold client money unless working in an authorised body (Paragraph 4.3).

Equally, there is a presumption of undue influence where a fiduciary duty exists. This means that in any dealings between a solicitor and the client, there will be a rebuttable presumption that the solicitor has exercised undue influence in persuading the client to enter into that dealing. In order to rebut this presumption, the solicitor would need to show that such influence had not been exercised, for example by making a full disclosure of all relevant facts, ensuring that the client took independent legal advice and understood the transaction, and ensuring that all dealings were fair and at arm's length.

4.4.3 Duty not to take advantage of the client

As a result of the fiduciary relationship between the solicitor and client, the solicitor must not take advantage of the client. This is reflected in Principle 5, which provides that a solicitor must act with integrity, and in Paragraph 1.2: 'You [must] not abuse your position by taking unfair advantage of clients or others.'

4.4.4 Confidentiality

A solicitor has a duty to keep the affairs of the client confidential (see **Chapter 6**). This duty continues even after the retainer has been terminated.

4.4.5 Disclosure

A solicitor owes the client a duty to disclose all relevant information to the client, regardless of the source of this information (see **Chapter 6**).

4.4.6 Client care and costs

A solicitor is obliged to provide information on costs (at the time of engagement and, when appropriate, as the client's matter progresses) and other information to enable the client to make informed decisions. A solicitor must also deal with the client's matter in a competent and timely manner and taking account of the client's attributes, needs and circumstances (see **Chapter 5**).

4.5 The client's authority

A solicitor may derive authority from the retainer to bind the client in certain circumstances. This authority can be limited expressly by the client in the terms of the retainer. However, the solicitor should never seek to rely on this implied authority to bind the client. Express instructions should always be taken from the client prior to the solicitor taking any step in the proceedings or matter.

4.6   Termination of the retainer

As with any contractual relationship, the retainer may be terminated by either party, or by the general law.

4.6.1   Termination by the client

A client may terminate the retainer at any time for any reason. However, the client is likely to be liable to pay the solicitor's fees for work done up until the point of termination. A solicitor may require their costs to be paid prior to forwarding the file to the client.

4.6.2   Termination by the solicitor

In contrast to the right of a client to terminate the retainer at will, a solicitor must consider whether the solicitor will be able to justify a decision to terminate the retainer having regard to their obligations under the SRA's regulatory arrangements (including the Principles and the Code of Conduct for Solicitors) (Paragraph 7.2). Good reasons for terminating the retainer may include:

(a) complying with the client's instructions would involve the solicitor in a breach of the law or the requirements of professional conduct;

(b) the solicitor cannot obtain proper instructions from the client;

(c) there has been a breakdown in confidence within the relationship between the solicitor and client (eg the client is not willing to accept the advice of the solicitor).

Good practice dictates that a client be provided with reasonable notice of termination. As to what would amount to reasonable notice will depend on the circumstances. For example, it is unlikely to be acceptable to stop acting for the client immediately before a court hearing, where it would be impossible for the client to find other representation at the hearing.

4.6.3   Termination by law

The retainer will be terminated automatically by law in certain circumstances. These include where the solicitor is declared bankrupt or either party loses mental capacity after the retainer has commenced.

Where the solicitor does not practise as a sole practitioner, being declared bankrupt or losing mental capacity will have little practical effect, as one of the solicitor's partners or other colleagues will take over the client's matter.

Where the client loses mental capacity, the solicitor should have regard to the Mental Capacity Act 2005 and its accompanying Code.

4.6.4   Responsibilities on termination

As a matter of good practice, a solicitor should confirm to the client in writing that the retainer has been terminated, explain, where appropriate, the client's possible options for pursuing the matter and take steps to deal with any property of the client which may be held by the solicitor. For example, the solicitor may be holding client monies which, subject to the position on costs, should be returned to the client as soon as possible, together with any interest.

The solicitor will also have to deal with the client's paperwork. Where the client's matter is ongoing and the client has instructed another firm of solicitors, it may be advisable to retain a copy of the file. The solicitor should also consider the client's rights and the solicitor's obligations under the Data Protection Act 2018. The Act requires that any personal data in those files are retained only for the purpose for which they were collected, although this will not prevent the solicitor from retaining a copy of the file in order to defend themselves from any future claims of negligence.

⭐ *Example*

Jay is a solicitor. Jay has acted for Ms Caldicott for a number of years, and Jay considers her to be a good client. Jay is currently dealing with the sale of one of Ms Caldicott's businesses. Ms Caldicott contacts Jay to express her disappointment that Jay's firm has recently been acting in defence of a large corporation accused of polluting a local river. On this basis Ms Caldicott demands that Jay transfer her files to another firm of solicitors. Jay does not consider that he has done anything wrong.

Can Jay stop Ms Caldicott transferring to other solicitors?

No. A client has the right to terminate the retainer at any time and for any reason.

4.7   Liens

A lien is a legal right that allows a creditor to retain a debtor's property until payment. Accordingly, a solicitor may hold on to property already in their possession, such as a client's papers, until the solicitor's proper fees are paid. Although a solicitor may accept an undertaking to pay the costs instead of the solicitor retaining the client's papers under a lien.

The court has the power under s 68 Solicitors Act 1974 to order the solicitor to deliver up any papers to the client. The SRA also has a similar power where it has intervened in a solicitor's practice.

Alternatively, a solicitor may apply to court under s 73 Solicitors Act 1974 for a charging order over any personal property of the client recovered or preserved by the solicitor within litigation proceedings. The charging order may cover the solicitor's taxed costs for those proceedings.

Summary

- The solicitor must ensure that the client understands the extent of the retainer between the solicitor and client.

- The solicitor must only act for clients on the instructions from the client, or someone properly authorised to provide instructions on their behalf. If the solicitor has reason to suspect that the instructions do not represent the client's wishes, the solicitor should take steps to satisfy themselves that they do.

- A solicitor's ability to accept or decline instructions is limited by the general law and the requirements of professional conduct.

- A solicitor must not unfairly discriminate when refusing instructions to act for a client.

- The solicitor has a duty to act with reasonable skill and care when providing services (such as legal advice).

- The solicitor has a fiduciary duty to act in the best interests of the client. Accordingly, a solicitor must not take advantage of the client.

- A solicitor owes various duties to the client throughout the retainer, including a duty of confidentiality and a duty of disclosure.

- A solicitor should not seek to rely on any implied authority to bind the client.

- The retainer may be terminated by either party, or by law.

- The solicitor's right to terminate the retainer is restricted by the law and the requirements of professional conduct.

- As a matter of good practice, a solicitor should deal promptly with the papers and property of the client within the solicitor's possession. In certain circumstances a solicitor may exercise a lien over this property until their fees are paid.

Sample questions

Question 1

A solicitor is instructed by a long-standing client to draw up the client's will. The client's instructions are that, in recognition of all the work the solicitor has done for the client over the years, the will is to include a legacy of £10,000 to the solicitor.

Which of the following best describes what the solicitor should do?

A   Refuse to draw up the will.

B   Draw up the will, but omit the legacy.

C   Draw up the will, as instructed, after the client has taken independent advice.

D   Draw up the will, but make the legacy payable to the solicitor's children.

E   Draw up the will, as instructed, after giving the client the details of local solicitors able to advise on wills.

Answer

Option C is correct. The guidance from the SRA is that usually a solicitor should refuse to act where the client is proposing to make a significant gift to the solicitor or a family member etc unless the solicitor is satisfied that the client has taken independent advice. It is not sufficient simply to give the client details of other solicitors (option E is wrong). The solicitor should not take it upon themselves to deviate from the client's express instructions (options B and D are wrong). Option A is wrong because it would be premature to refuse to draw up the will at this stage – the client's instructions can be accommodated if the client agrees to take independent advice.

Question 2

A father and daughter are buying a property together. The daughter instructs a solicitor to deal with the purchase on their joint behalf. The daughter explains that the father is elderly and too frail to attend at the solicitor's office. The daughter tells the solicitor that the property is to be held by them as beneficial joint tenants, but that the father will be providing all the money for the purchase price. The daughter says that they are buying the property so that the daughter can move in to live with the father and care for him in his old age.

Should the solicitor act on the daughter's instructions and immediately proceed with the purchase?

A   No, because a solicitor cannot accept instructions from a third party in any circumstances.

B   No, because the solicitor has reason to suspect that the instructions do not represent the father's wishes.

C   Yes, because the daughter alone is the client.

D Yes, because proceeding with the purchase is in the father's best interests.

E Yes, because, as the father's carer, the daughter is automatically authorised to give instructions on his behalf.

Answer

Option B is the best answer. The solicitor is being instructed by joint purchasers (option C is wrong). The solicitor can accept instructions from a third party who is authorised to give those instructions (option A therefore overstates the matter). However, the daughter's status as a carer would not give her that authority (option E is therefore wrong). The father's age, frailty and the fact that he alone is providing the entire purchase price mean that there is reason to suspect that the instructions do not represent the father's wishes (option D therefore does not represent the best answer). The solicitor should not proceed until they have satisfied themselves that the instructions do accord with the father's wishes. The solicitor cannot establish that the purchase is in the father's best interests until the father's wishes are established.

Question 3

A female solicitor is instructed by a male client in an acrimonious litigation matter. The case progresses properly for two months. Then the solicitor receives a letter from the client saying that the client has come to the view that women are too weak for robust litigation. The client goes on to say that he has now instructed a male solicitor in a different firm. The client asks for his file to be transferred to his new solicitor without delay.

On looking at the client's file the solicitor sees that there are fees outstanding of £2,000 for the work that the she has completed to date on the case.

Which of the following best describes the professional conduct position?

A The client cannot terminate the retainer because his grounds are discriminatory.

B The solicitor can retain the file until her proper fees are paid.

C The client cannot terminate the retainer because the solicitor has dealt with the case properly to date.

D The solicitor must transfer the file to the new solicitor immediately, but is entitled to be paid her proper fees.

E The client cannot terminate the retainer because he has not given reasonable notice to the solicitor.

Answer

Option B is correct. The solicitor has a lien over the file until her proper fees are paid. Option D is wrong because the solicitor is under no obligation to hand the file over until payment unless ordered to do so by the court (although the solicitor may agree to hand over the file). Options A, C and E are wrong – a client has the right to terminate the retainer at any time and for any reason.

5 Client Care and Costs

SQE1 syllabus

This chapter will help you to achieve the SQE1 Assessment Specification in relation to Functioning Legal Knowledge concerned with Ethics and Professional Conduct on:

- the purpose, scope and content of the SRA Principles,
- the purpose, scope and content of the SRA Code of Conduct for Solicitors, RELs and RFLS.

Ethics and Professional Conduct is a pervasive topic in SQE1 and may be examined across all subject areas.

Note that for SQE1, candidates are not usually required to recall specific case names or cite statutory or regulatory authorities. Cases are provided for illustrative purposes only.

Learning outcomes

By the end of this chapter you will be able to demonstrate your ability to act honestly and with integrity, and in accordance with the SRA Standards and Regulations in relation to:

- maintain trust and acting fairly;
- service and competence;
- client information and publicity; and
- client money and assets.

5.1 Introduction

The marketplace for legal services is a very competitive area. From high street practitioners to global law firms, the competition to work for the best clients in a particular matter is often fierce. Firms often spend large amounts of money on marketing budgets to attract clients. It is therefore in a firm's best interests to try to keep their clients from instructing other firms by providing a high level of service.

This chapter looks at:

- client care
- information about costs
- client care letter
- Consumer Contract Regulations 2013
- fees and costs
- options available for solicitors' fees
- money on account
- the solicitor's bill
- the client's right to challenge the bill
- non-contentious business agreements
- contentious business agreements
- overcharging
- commission.

5.2 Client care

The Code of Conduct for Solicitors sets out the minimum standards of service and competence that a client can expect to receive. This links to Principle 7: a solicitor must act in the best interests of each client. This includes providing a proper standard of service. More generally, the Code provides that a solicitor must not abuse their position by taking advantage of clients (Paragraph 1.2) or mislead or attempt to mislead a client either by their own acts or omissions or allowing or being complicit in the acts or omissions of others (Paragraph 1.4).

The Code of Conduct for Solicitors is not prescriptive on how a solicitor should comply with the obligations relating to a standard of service, as different types of legal services providers will have in place differing client care systems. Also, the introduction to the Code makes clear that a solicitor must exercise their own judgment in applying the standards, bearing in mind the solicitor's areas of practice and the nature of the solicitor's clients. So, for example, a client providing instructions on a conveyancing matter is unlikely to need the same information as a sophisticated commercial client who instructs the solicitor on a regular basis.

5.2.1 Making informed decisions

A solicitor must give clients information in a way they can understand and ensure that clients are in a position to make informed decisions about the services they need, how their matter will be handled and the options available to them (Paragraph 8.6).

As part of this process, therefore, it may be appropriate for the solicitor, for example, to discuss whether the potential outcomes of the client's matter are likely to justify the expense or risk involved, including any risk of having to pay someone else's legal fees. A common complaint from clients is that they were unaware that it would cost so much to achieve so little.

5.2.2 Level of service

The service provided by a solicitor must be competent and delivered in a timely manner (Paragraph 3.2). A solicitor must maintain their competence to carry out their role and keep their professional knowledge and skills up to date (Paragraph 3.3).

In seeking to achieve a competent level of service, the solicitor must consider and take account of the client's attributes, needs and circumstances (Paragraph 3.4). For example, in terms of the type and frequency of communications with a client during the matter, some clients may want to be updated in writing on a regular basis, whilst some may want to hear nothing from a solicitor until a certain stage of a transaction has been reached.

5.2.3 Responsibilities

Both the solicitor and client will have their own responsibilities during the conduct of the client's matter, and so it is good practice to ensure that these responsibilities are explained and agreed with the client at the outset and prudent to have a written record of this. For example, one of the responsibilities of the solicitor could be to keep the client informed of progress and seek the client's instructions where required. The solicitor will also expect the client to keep the solicitor updated as the matter progresses and inform the solicitor of anything that occurs which may materially affect the matter or change the basis of the client's instructions.

Where a client has been referred to the solicitor by a third party and/or because of the way the client's matter is funded, there may be conditions placed on how the solicitor may act for the client. For example, a client may be referred to a solicitor by the client's insurer. Under the terms of acting, the solicitor may not be able to issue proceedings without the authority of the insurer (who will be funding any such action). Accordingly, it is important that the solicitor explains at the outset and throughout the matter any limitations or conditions on what the solicitor can do for the client for the avoidance of any misunderstanding or potential source of grievance on the part of the client.

5.2.4 Competence and supervision

In order to provide a proper level of service to clients, it is obvious that a solicitor should have a knowledge of the current law and the skills to enable the solicitor to carry out their role effectively. Accordingly, the Code of Conduct for Solicitors provides that a solicitor must maintain their competence to carry out their role and keep their professional knowledge and skills up to date (Paragraph 3.3).

It is important not only that the particular solicitor provides a competent level of service to clients, but also that the solicitor ensures that those they supervise or manage do so too. As a result, the Code of Conduct for Solicitors obliges a solicitor to ensure that the individuals they manage are competent to carry out their role and keep their professional knowledge and skills, as well as an understanding of their legal, ethical and regulatory obligations, up to date (Paragraph 3.6). The Code also makes it clear that a solicitor, when supervising or managing others providing legal services, remains accountable for the work carried out through them and must effectively supervise work they do for clients (Paragraph 3.5).

5.2.5 Information on regulation

A solicitor must ensure that clients understand whether and how the services being provided are regulated. This includes the solicitor explaining which activities will be carried out by the solicitor as an 'authorised person' (defined in the SRA Glossary as a person who is authorised by the SRA or another approved regulator to carry out a legal activity as set out in s 12 of the Legal Services Act 2007), which services being provided are regulated by an approved regulator, and ensuring that the solicitor does not represent any business or employer which is not authorised by the SRA as being regulated by the SRA (Paragraph 8.10).

There is also an obligation to ensure that clients understand the regulatory protections available to them (Paragraph 8.11); for example, entitlement to the protection of the SRA Compensation Fund (see **1.10**) and the firm's indemnity insurance.

For solicitors, the regulator will be the SRA and, in some circumstances, the Financial Conduct Authority.

5.3 Information about costs

One of the most important issues for a client is the overall cost of legal services. When an individual goes into a shop to buy something, it is easy for them to work out how much the thing will cost and therefore whether they want to spend that amount of money on buying the product.

The provision of legal services often does not work in the same way. Nevertheless, the client must be given the best possible information as to the overall costs of the matter if the client is to be able to make an informed decision about whether they want to proceed. As the Legal Ombudsman puts it, 'A client should never be surprised by the bill they receive from a lawyer.' (*An Ombudsman's View of Good Costs Service*, 3rd edn)

5.3.1 Best possible information

A solicitor is obliged to provide clients with the best possible information about how their matter will be priced and, both at the time of engagement and when appropriate as their matter progresses, about the likely overall cost of a matter and any costs incurred (Paragraph 8.7). The term 'costs' is defined in the SRA Glossary as meaning the solicitor's fees and disbursements.

Care must be taken in providing an accurate costs estimate. Aside from the professional conduct implications, it may be the case that the solicitor will be held to the estimate:

Reynolds v Stone Rowe Brewer [2008] EWHC 497 (QB)

The case concerned a dispute between the client and a building contractor about some work carried out at the client's properties. At the outset the solicitor said that the costs of taking the matter to trial would be £10,000 to £18,000. A few months later, the solicitor said that their revised estimate was now £30,000.

The court found that the revised estimate was an attempt to correct an underestimate and was not justified by any change in the facts. There had been no unusual developments in the case so as to justify the difference between the two estimates. The court held that the firm was bound by the original estimate.

Despite the requirement in Paragraph 8.7, a lack of clarity about costs is one of the most common causes of complaints to the Legal Ombudsman (see **1.5**) Recently, a number of such complainants have been able to demonstrate that their legal fees were either unfairly high or had not been made clear to them and, as a result, have succeeded in obtaining a refund. The Legal Ombudsman notes the importance of a client being 'fully involved' with costs and understanding what they would or might have to pay ('Complaints about legal costs – what legal providers, consumers and their representatives need to know', October 2024).

There is no specific guidance in the Code of Conduct for Solicitors as to what will constitute 'the best possible information' about costs, as, again, the intention is for a solicitor to exercise their own judgment in applying the standards, taking into account their areas of practice and the nature of their clients. As a matter of good practice, however, the solicitor should clearly explain how fees are calculated and if and when they are likely to change. For example, the client may be charged a fixed fee, or by reference to an hourly charge-out rate. Warning the client about any other payments for which the client will or may be responsible is also essential. For example, in a residential conveyancing matter, the solicitor will be obliged to pay for searches from the Land Registry and others; in a litigation matter there may be court fees and counsel's fees to be paid.

It will often be impossible to provide an accurate figure for the overall cost of a matter at the start. However, just providing the client with details of the solicitor's charge-out rate will rarely be sufficient. For example, if the only information the solicitor provides to a client is that the solicitor's charge-out rate will be £300 per hour, the client will not know whether they will have to pay £300 for the matter to be finished (if the solicitor puts in one hour's work) or £30,000 (if the solicitor puts in 100 hours' work). The solicitor should provide a reasonable estimate or at least a costs range. In order to make an informed decision about whether to proceed with their case, a client must understand how much they can expect to pay for it to be completed.

If a precise figure is genuinely not possible, it will often be prudent for the solicitor to explain why the precise figure cannot be given and agree either:

(a) a ceiling figure, above which the solicitor's costs cannot go, without the client's permission; or

(b) a review date when the parties will revisit the costs position.

The solicitor must not forget expressly to include VAT in any hourly rate or quote. For example, a solicitor may quote the hourly rate as £300 plus VAT. If the solicitor fails to quote with VAT, the price the client pays will be deemed to include VAT. Accordingly, if a solicitor were to say that their charge-out rate was £300 per hour that is all that the client would be liable to pay. The solicitor would have to pay the VAT element to HM Revenue and Customs from this £300, and would therefore lose out.

In seeking to provide clients with a competent service, the solicitor should discuss how the client will pay for the legal services, including whether the client may be able to have some or all of the costs covered by someone else, such as a trade union, or by legal expenses insurance. Consideration should also be given, where appropriate, as to whether the client may be eligible for legal aid and, if so, how this would operate.

The SRA Transparency Rules impose additional obligations on solicitors and firms in providing costs information (see **3.3.3.2**).

5.3.2 Costs issues in litigation

Providing a competent level of service is likely to include the solicitor discussing with the client whether the potential outcomes of the matter are likely to justify the expense or risk involved. This would include discussing any risk of having to pay someone else's legal fees. For example, in litigation the client may be ordered to pay some of the costs of the winning party. The solicitor should consider whether these costs might be covered by legal expenses insurance.

Regardless of success in litigation, the client must be advised that they may still be liable to pay their own solicitor's costs. For example, the amount that the losing party in litigation has to pay to the winning party will be assessed by the court or subject to the fixed recoverable costs regime, and it is unlikely to cover the entirety of the winning client's legal costs. The client must know the circumstances in which they will be responsible for the shortfall.

The client will also remain liable to pay their solicitor's costs where the losing party is unable to meet the costs order. Again, this must be made clear to the client prior to starting any litigious proceedings.

Specific obligations relating to providing costs information in the context of certain court or tribunal proceedings are contained in the SRA Transparency Rules (see **3.3.3.2**).

5.4 Client care letter

There is a good deal of client care information which will need to be communicated to the client at the start of the matter. Some of this information is prescribed by the Code of Conduct for Solicitors (eg information on costs and complaints), some by other rules and regulations (eg the Consumer Contract Regulations 2013) and some simply as a matter of good practice.

It is prudent for a solicitor to provide the necessary client care information to a client in writing, and traditionally this has been done in the form of a letter sent out to the client after the first interview, known as the 'client care letter'.

Although not a specific requirement under the Code of Conduct for Solicitors, most solicitors continue to provide the client care information and the terms of the firm's retainer in the form of a letter (or electronic equivalent) to the client for the avoidance of doubt, and to help show compliance generally with the Code and the Principles.

The solicitor must keep in mind the requirement to give clients information in a way they can understand (Paragraph 8.6). So even though the letter will in part be intended to impart technical information and demonstrate the solicitor's compliance with various requirements, its primary purpose is to inform the client. The letter must therefore be written in a client friendly way.

5.5 Consumer Contracts Regulations 2013

Solicitors need to ensure that they comply with the Consumer Contracts (Information, Cancellation and Additional Charges) Regulations 2013 (SI 2013/3134). These apply to a wide range of contracts made between solicitors and their clients and would include a contract to carry out legal work for a client. The Regulations distinguish between 'on-premises' and 'off-premises' contracts. Whilst most contracts will be concluded between a solicitor and the client at the solicitor's place of business ('on-premises'), there may be situations which will result in the contract falling within the definition of an 'off-premises' contract, for example where a solicitor visits a client at home and the client offers to engage the solicitor to carry out legal work. Even if the offer is accepted by the solicitor telephoning the client from the solicitor's office the next day, this would be considered an 'off-premises' contract.

The Regulations specify that certain pieces of information must be provided to clients before they enter into the contract. Much of the information that solicitors are required to provide under the Regulations is likely to be included in their client care letter. However, the information required varies depending on the type of contract. For example, where a client has agreed to an 'off-premises' contract, the client must additionally be informed that they have the right to cancel it without giving any reason or incurring any liability during the cancellation period (which in most cases is 14 days beginning on the date after the contract is entered into). Failure to do so is an offence under the Regulations. For this reason, solicitors need to ensure that if they are likely to enter into contracts in different types of circumstances, their standard letters contain any additional information required under the Regulations. Legal aid contracts do not fall within the Regulations.

5.6 Fees and costs

The retainer between the solicitor and client is a contract, and so the fees and charges the solicitor will levy for acting for the client will be agreed between the parties at the start of the retainer. However, restrictions are placed upon the fees a solicitor may charge, and also upon how the solicitor will be remunerated by the SRA and the general law. Below is a summary of the main provisions; it is not intended to be a comprehensive guide.

These restrictions vary depending upon what type of work the solicitor has agreed to carry out for the client. A distinction is made between 'contentious' business and 'non-contentious' business. This distinction is particularly relevant when considering whether, and how, a client can challenge the bill of a solicitor. It should be noted that this distinction has been subject to judicial criticism and described as artificial and out of step with modern business practices (see *Belsner v Cam Legal Services* [2022] EWCA Civ 1387).

5.6.1 Contentious business

Contentious business is defined as 'business done, whether as a solicitor or an advocate, in or for the purposes of proceedings begun before a court or an arbitrator, not being business which falls within the definition of non-contentious business or common form probate business' (Solicitors Act 1974, s 87). Accordingly, contentious business is work done in relation to proceedings. However, contentious business starts only once proceedings have been issued.

For example, a client may seek the advice of a solicitor with a view to suing the client's previous firm of solicitors for negligence. The solicitor advises that the client should start proceedings, but suggests that a letter is sent to the previous firm beforehand, giving that firm seven days to offer appropriate compensation. The client is clearly contemplating litigious proceedings, but if the firm makes an acceptable offer before proceedings are issued, the solicitor's work will be classified as non-contentious.

5.6.2 Non-contentious business

Non-contentious business is defined as 'any business done as a solicitor which is not contentious business' (Solicitors Act 1974, s 87). This includes obvious examples such as conveyancing or commercial drafting work. The definition also includes all proceedings before tribunals, except the Lands Tribunal and the Employment Appeals Tribunal.

Non-contentious business is governed by the Solicitors' (Non-Contentious Business) Remuneration Order 2009 (SI 2009/1931).

5.7 Options available for solicitors' fees

A solicitor may agree to charge a client for work done on a number of different bases. Some of these options are considered below (funding options are dealt with in more detail in **Legal Services**). Whichever method of charging the client and solicitor agree, the overall amount of the charge will be regulated by statute and so the client may be able to challenge the bill at a later date. A solicitor is required to ensure that clients receive the best possible information about how their matter will be priced (Paragraph 8.7).

5.7.1 Hourly rate

A common method of charging clients is by use of an hourly rate, that is, the client is charged for the time spent on the file. The client is informed at the start of the matter which fee earner will be working on the client's files, and the fee earner's respective charge-out rates. However, in order to ensure that the client receives the best possible information about the likely overall cost of the matter (Paragraph 8.7), it is unlikely that merely giving an hourly rate will be sufficient.

5.7.2 Fixed fees

A solicitor may agree with the client to complete the work for a fixed fee, or a fixed fee plus VAT and disbursements. Fixed fees are often used for conveyancing transactions. If the solicitor agrees to act in return for a fixed fee, this fee cannot be altered at a later date (unless the client agrees) if the work turns out to be more expensive than the solicitor first expected.

5.7.3 Variable fees

A solicitor is permitted, in certain circumstances, to charge a fee which varies according to the outcome of the matter. One such example of a variable fee is a contingency fee. However, a solicitor must bear in mind the obligation to take account of the client's needs and circumstances (Paragraph 3.4) when deciding to enter into fee agreements and to ensure that any such agreements are legal.

Agreements which are permitted by law are conditional fee agreements (CFAs) and damages-based agreements (DBAs). An example of a conditional fee agreement is the 'no win, no fee' basis of charging that is popular in areas of work such as personal injury. Under such an agreement, the solicitor may agree to charge nothing if the client loses, but will charge their fees plus an agreed 'uplift' (or 'success fee', for example an extra 20%) in the event of success.

In respect of litigation or advocacy services, a solicitor may enter into (and enforce) a CFA if it complies with s 58 Courts and Legal Services Act 1990 (see also the Conditional Fee Agreements Order 2013 (SI 2013/689)). For example, the agreement must be in writing, signed by both the solicitor and the client, and, where a success fee is to be paid, specify the percentage of the success fee. The success fee cannot exceed a percentage specified by the Lord Chancellor (currently 100% uplift in the normal hourly charge rate, with the exception of personal injury cases where the cap is 25% of general damages recovered). The solicitor must carry out a proper risk assessment to calculate the amount of the success fee. A solicitor cannot enter into a CFA for any criminal work or family proceedings.

The CFA must also comply with the additional requirements specified by the Consumer Contracts (Information, Cancellation and Additional Charges) Regulations 2013.

If a client instructs a solicitor on a CFA, this does not mean that the client will not have to pay any legal costs if the client loses the case. Although the client may not be liable to pay their solicitor's fees, they will usually have to pay disbursements such as court fees, barristers' fees and VAT. The client may also have to pay the opponent's costs. A solicitor should explore whether the client can obtain insurance to cover these costs in the event of losing the case (known as after-the-event insurance). The solicitor should also ask whether the client has before-the-event insurance which will cover the costs.

A DBA (defined by s 58AA(3)(a) Courts and Legal Services Act 1990 and covered by the Damages-Based Agreements Regulations 2013 (SI 2013/609)) provides that, if the client recovers damages, the solicitor's fee is an agreed percentage of those damages. The DBA must not provide for a payment above an amount which, including VAT, is equal to 50% of the sums ultimately recovered by the client. Also, personal injury cases are subject to a cap of 25% of the general damages recovered. The points made above in respect of combining a CFA with after-the-event insurance cover (or before-the-event insurance cover) apply equally to a DBA.

The SRA Transparency Rules (see **3.3.3.2**) also require that, in relation to specified services, costs information required to be published includes the circumstances in which clients may have to make any payments themselves for the services provided by the solicitor (including from any damages) if CFAs or DBAs are used.

A solicitor may enter into a contingency fee arrangement in respect of non-contentious work, but to be enforceable this must be in the form of a non-contentious business agreement.

5.7.4 Other methods

A solicitor may agree to be remunerated by some other means. One such example would be a solicitor agreeing to accept shares in a new company in return for the work, rather than costs. However, in such circumstances the client should be advised to seek independent advice about such a costs agreement.

5.8 Money on account

It is common for a solicitor to require a client to pay a sum of money to the solicitor at the start of the transaction on account of the costs and disbursements that will be incurred.

In contentious business, a solicitor may require a client to pay a reasonable sum to the solicitor on account of costs. If the client does not pay this money within a reasonable time, the solicitor may terminate the retainer (Solicitors Act 1974, s 65(2)).

There is no such statutory right in non-contentious business. Accordingly, where the solicitor requires money on account before starting a matter, the solicitor should make this a requirement of the retainer.

5.9 The solicitor's bill

For a solicitor to be able to obtain payment from the client, certain formalities need to be complied with in respect of the solicitor's bill. These matters include (but are not limited to) the following:

(a) The bill must contain enough information for the client to be satisfied that the bill is reasonable, and also provide details of the period to which the bill relates.

(b) The bill must be signed by the solicitor or on the solicitor's behalf by an employee authorised to do so. Alternatively, the solicitor/authorised employee may sign a covering letter which refers to the bill (Solicitors Act 1974, s 69(2A)).

(c) The bill must be delivered by hand to the client, by post to the client's home, business address or last known address, or by email if the client has agreed to this method and provided an appropriate email address (Solicitors Act 1974, s 69(2C)).

5.9.1 Interim bills

A solicitor may wish to bill the client for work done on the client's file before the matter has completed. This will particularly be the case where the client's matter is likely to go on for some months, such as protracted litigation. A solicitor may wish to issue interim bills throughout the matter.

There are two different types of interim bills. The first type are known as interim 'statute bills' because they comply with the provisions of the Solicitors Act 1974. Although they are interim bills, they are also self-contained final bills in respect of the work covered by them. Consequently, the solicitor may sue the client for non-payment of such bills and the client may apply to have them assessed by the court. However, interim statute bills are rare and may arise during the retainer in only two ways:

(a) there is authority for issuing such bills in a 'natural break' in lengthy proceedings, but there is little authority as to what will actually amount to a natural break, and so this should perhaps be avoided as a basis for statute bills except in the clearest of cases;

(b) by agreement with the client, and the Law Society recommends that this right should be expressly reserved within the retainer. The Law Society's guidance provides that the solicitor must specify the time-limit within which the client must pay the interim bill, and must also expressly reserve the right to terminate the retainer in the event of non-payment.

The second, and more common, type of interim bill is the 'bill on account'. Such bills are effectively requests for payments on account of the final bill which will be delivered at the end of the matter/retainer. An advantage of this type of interim bill is that it does not need to represent the final figure for costs in respect of the work covered by it, so that when preparing the statute bill at the end of the matter the solicitor can assess a fair overall costs figure for all of the work done since the start of the retainer. However, unlike with an interim statute bill, a solicitor is unable to sue the client for non-payment of such a bill, and the client cannot apply to have the bill assessed. If the client does not pay the bill on account within a reasonable time then in contentious business the solicitor may terminate the retainer under s 65(2)

Solicitors Act 1974. In the event that the client regards the amount of the bill as excessive, the client can request that the solicitor issues a statute bill which the client may then apply to have assessed by the court.

5.9.2 Interest on bills

In a non-contentious matter a solicitor may charge interest on the whole or the outstanding part of an unpaid bill with effect from one month after delivery of the bill, provided that the client has been given notice of their right to challenge the bill. The rate of interest chargeable must not exceed that which is payable on judgment debts. At the time of writing the rate is 8%.

In contentious business, the Law Society's guidance provides that a solicitor may charge interest on an unpaid bill where the solicitor expressly reserves this right in the retainer, or the client later agrees for a 'contractual consideration' to pay interest. Alternatively, where a solicitor sues the client for non-payment of fees, the court has the power to award the solicitor interest on the debt under s 35A of the Senior Courts Act 1981 or s 69 of the County Courts Act 1984.

The rate of interest will be the rate payable for judgment debts unless the solicitor and client expressly agree a different rate.

5.9.3 Enforcement

Subject to certain exceptions, a solicitor may not commence any claim to recover any costs due to the solicitor (such as suing the client) until one month has passed since the solicitor delivered their bill (Solicitors Act 1974, s 69). The bill must also be in the proper form.

However, the High Court has the power under s 69 to allow the solicitor to commence such a claim against the client within this one-month period where the court is satisfied that the client is about to leave the country, be declared bankrupt (or enter into a composition with their creditors), or do anything else which would prevent or delay the solicitor obtaining their fees.

5.10 The client's right to challenge the bill

The client may challenge the amount of a solicitor's bill, provided that the client complies with certain requirements. These requirements depend upon how the client wishes to go about challenging the bill.

5.10.1 Assessment by the court

A client may apply to have the bill assessed by the court in both contentious and non-contentious proceedings. This is sometimes referred to as a bill being 'taxed'.

A client has the right to have a bill assessed if an application is made to the court within one month of delivery of the bill. Where no such application has been made within this month, the court still has the power to order assessment within 12 months of delivery of the bill, or even after this time if the client can show special circumstances. However, assessment is not permitted if more than 12 months have expired since payment of the bill. 'Payment' in this context requires the client's acceptance of and agreement to the amount charged (*Oakwood Solicitors Ltd v Menzies* [2024] UKSC 34).

The costs will be assessed by a judge or district judge sitting as a 'costs officer'. The costs officer has the power to assess the fees and disbursements of the solicitor.

The costs will (with certain exceptions) be assessed on an 'indemnity basis'. The court will allow only costs that have been reasonably incurred by the solicitor and which are reasonable in amount. Any doubt as to what is to be considered reasonable is resolved in favour of the solicitor. However, the client may be ordered to pay the costs of the solicitor arising from the assessment process.

5.10.1.1 Non-contentious proceedings

Where a court is asked to assess a solicitor's bill in non-contentious proceedings, in deciding what is reasonable, the court must have regard to the following circumstances (Solicitors' (Non-Contentious Business) Remuneration Order 2009):

(a) the complexity of the matter, or the difficulty or novelty of the questions raised;

(b) the skill, labour, specialised knowledge and responsibility involved;

(c) the time spent on the business;

(d) the number and importance of the documents prepared or considered, without regard to length;

(e) the place where and the circumstances in which the business or any part thereof is transacted;

(f) the amount or value of any money or property involved;

(g) whether any land involved is registered;

(h) the importance of the matter to the client; and

(i) the approval (express or implied) of the entitled person, or the express approval of the testator, to:

(i) the solicitor undertaking all or any part of the work giving rise to the costs, or

(ii) the amount of the costs.

5.10.1.2 Contentious proceedings

The factors the court must take into account when considering whether costs are reasonable are set out in r 44.5 Civil Procedure Rules. These include (but are not limited to):

(a) the conduct of the parties;

(b) the amount or value of any money or property involved;

(c) the importance of the matter to the parties;

(d) the particular complexity of the matter, or the difficulty or novelty of the questions raised;

(e) the skill, effort, specialised knowledge and responsibility involved;

(f) the time spent on the case; and

(g) the place where and the circumstances in which work, or any part of it, was done.

Subject to certain exceptions, a client cannot apply for an assessment of costs where the solicitor and client have entered into a contentious business agreement.

5.10.2 Using the firm's complaints procedure

Solicitors must ensure that clients are informed in writing at the time of engagement about their right to complain about the service provided by them and their charges (Paragraph 8.3).

If the client is not satisfied with the firm's response, the solicitor must inform the client in writing of any right the client has to complain to the Legal Ombudsman (Paragraph 8.4). The Legal Ombudsman may then limit the solicitor's fees by, for example, directing the solicitor to refund all or part of any amount paid, or to remit all or part of the fees (see **1.5**).

⭐ *Example*

> *Rex has just received a final bill from his solicitor in respect of a partnership dispute. The dispute was resolved without having to issue proceedings. Rex thinks that the bill (£7,000 plus VAT) is too high.*
>
> *Assuming that the bill complies with the relevant formalities, what options are available to Rex to challenge the bill?*

Rex has two options:

(a) Assessment by the court

> *Rex has the right to have the bill assessed by the court if he applies within one month of delivery of the bill (the court may allow assessment after this time in certain circumstances). Both Rex and the solicitor will be bound by the results.*

(b) Using the firm's complaints procedure

> *Rex could make a formal complaint about the bill in accordance with the firm's complaints procedure. If he is not satisfied with the firm's response he may complain to the Legal Ombudsman (see 1.5). In the event that the Legal Ombudsman makes a determination about the bill (which can include a direction that the solicitor remits all or part of their fees) which is accepted by Rex, it will be binding on the solicitor.*

5.11 Non-contentious business agreements

A solicitor and client may enter into a non-contentious business agreement in respect of the solicitor's remuneration for any non-contentious work. Under this agreement the solicitor may be remunerated by a gross sum, commission, a percentage, a salary, or otherwise.

To be enforceable, the agreement must comply with s 57 Solicitors Act 1974. For example, the agreement must:

(a) be in writing;

(b) be signed by the client;

(c) contain all the terms of the agreement (including whether disbursements and VAT are included in the agreed remuneration).

Where the relevant provisions have been complied with, the client will be unable to apply to have the bill assessed by the court. However, the court may set the agreement aside if the amount charged by the solicitor is unfair or unreasonable.

5.12 Contentious business agreements

A solicitor may enter into a contentious business agreement in respect of their remuneration for contentious work completed on behalf of the client (Solicitors Act 1974, ss 59–63).

The agreement may provide for the solicitor to be remunerated by reference to a gross sum, an hourly rate, a salary or otherwise. However, the solicitor may not be remunerated by a contingency fee.

In order to be enforceable, the agreement must comply with certain requirements, including:

(a) the agreement must state it is a contentious business agreement;

(b) the agreement must be in writing;

(c) the agreement must be signed by the client; and

(d) the agreement must contain all the terms.

Where the contentious business agreement is enforceable, the client will be unable to apply to court for an assessment of costs (except where the agreement provides that the solicitor is to be remunerated by reference to an hourly rate). However, the court may set aside the agreement if it is unfair or unreasonable.

5.13 Overcharging

A solicitor must act in the best interests of the client (Principle 7) and act with integrity (Principle 5). Overcharging for work done would breach both these Principles. Where a costs officer (when assessing a solicitor's bill in a non-contentious matter) reduces the amount of the costs by more than 50%, they must inform the SRA.

5.14 Commission

The solicitor–client relationship is a fiduciary relationship (see **4.4**), and so a solicitor must not make a secret profit whilst acting for the client. Paragraph 4.1 obliges a solicitor to properly account to a client for any financial benefit the solicitor receives as a result of the client's instructions, except where they have agreed otherwise. The term 'financial benefit' includes any commission, discount or rebate (SRA Glossary).

For example, a client may require specialist tax advice, and so may be referred by the solicitor to a tax consultant. The tax consultant may pay the solicitor commission in return for this referral.

In showing that the solicitor has properly accounted to the client for the financial benefit received, the solicitor could:

(a) pay it to the client; or

(b) offset it against fees; or

(c) keep it where the client has agreed to this.

This is usually dealt with as part of the client care letter or the terms and conditions otherwise agreed upon in acting for the client.

Summary

- A solicitor must ensure that the service provided to clients is competent and delivered in a timely manner.

- The solicitor must ensure that clients are in a position to make informed decisions about the services they need, how their matter will be handled and the options available to them.

- The solicitor must inform clients in writing of their right to complain to the firm about the service they receive and the costs and any right they have to complain to the Legal Ombudsman, both at the time of engagement and at the conclusion of the firm's complaint procedure.

- A solicitor must not take unfair advantage of clients or mislead or attempt to mislead them.

- A solicitor must give the client the best possible information about how their matter will be priced and as to the likely overall costs of a matter and any costs incurred, both at the outset and when appropriate as the client's matter progresses.

- Information must be given in a way that clients can understand.

- A solicitor and client may agree the level of costs the solicitor may charge. However, this agreement is regulated by statute and the common law.

- A distinction is made between costs in contentious matters and costs in non-contentious matters.

- A solicitor's bill must contain prescribed information in order for the bill to be enforceable.

- A client may challenge the costs of a solicitor both in contentious and non-contentious proceedings.

- Generally, a solicitor may not sue to recover their costs from the client until one month has elapsed since the bill was delivered.

Sample questions

Question 1

A solicitor receives a telephone call from a client complaining about the bill which the solicitor sent to the client last week. The client wants the bill reduced, but the solicitor thinks that the bill is entirely justified.

Which of the following best describes what the solicitor should do?

A   Tell the client to take the complaint to the Legal Ombudsman.

B   Ask the court to assess the bill.

C   Refer the client to the firm's complaints procedure.

D   Warn the client that the firm will charge a set fee for dealing with the complaint.

E   Sue the client for the full amount of the bill.

Answer

Option C is correct. Complaints should be dealt with following the firm's complaints procedure (option A accordingly is not the best answer). It is only appropriate to involve the Legal Ombudsman if the complaint cannot be concluded to the client's satisfaction following the firm's complaints procedure. Complaints must be dealt with free of charge (option D is therefore wrong). Having costs assessed by the court is the right of the client, not the solicitor (option B is wrong). Option E is not the best answer as to sue the client is clearly premature.

Question 2

A solicitor is instructed by a new client in relation to an acrimonious divorce. The breakdown of the marriage is very recent and, when giving instructions at the first meeting with the solicitor, the client becomes distressed.

The solicitor's costs will be dealt with on the basis of an hourly charging rate. However, given the complexity of the case it is not possible for the solicitor to give an accurate figure for how much the case, as a whole, will cost.

Which of the following best describes how the solicitor should deal with the question of costs?

A   During the meeting the solicitor should give the client their hourly charging rate.

B   The solicitor should say nothing about costs as this will only cause the client more distress.

C   During the meeting the solicitor should tell the client about the hourly charging rate and warn that the overall cost will be high.

D   During the meeting the solicitor should tell the client about the hourly charging rate, explain the possible costs range and set a date for reviewing costs.

E   During the meeting the solicitor should explain that an accurate figure cannot be given for the overall cost of the case.

Answer

Option D is correct. Paragraph 8.7 requires the solicitor to ensure that the client receives the best possible information about how the matter will be priced and the likely overall cost of the matter. On these facts this would require the solicitor to explain the hourly charging rate as the basis of the charge (options B and E are therefore wrong). Additionally, as no accurate figure can be given for the overall costs, the solicitor should explain the costs range and set a date for reviewing costs (setting a costs ceiling would be an acceptable alternative). By simply referring to the hourly charging rate, option A does not go far enough. Finally, option C is not the best answer. Saying that the overall cost will be high is too vague and unhelpful to qualify as best possible information.

Question 3

A solicitor refers a client to a surveyor for advice on some structural damage to the client's property. This is the first client that the solicitor has referred to this particular surveyor. Following the referral the solicitor is surprised to receive £150 from the surveyor. The surveyor explains that their usual practice is to pay £150 commission for any referral as a gesture of goodwill.

Which of the following best explains what the solicitor should do about the £150?

A   There is no need to tell the client about the £150 because it is a private matter between the solicitor and the surveyor, so the solicitor can just keep the payment.

B   The solicitor must tell the client about the £150, but the solicitor is entitled to keep the payment because it was just a gesture of goodwill.

C   The solicitor must immediately return the £150 because solicitors are not permitted to receive commission fees under any circumstances.

D   The solicitor must tell the client about the £150, and keep the payment, if the client agrees.

E   The solicitor must immediately pay the £150 to the client.

Answer

Option D is correct. Paragraph 5.1 requires a solicitor to inform the client of *any* financial benefit the solicitor has in referring the client to another person. The client must therefore be told about the payment (option A is accordingly wrong). Paragraph 4.1 requires a solicitor to account to the client for any financial benefit received, unless the client agrees otherwise. Option B therefore is wrong in that the solicitor can only keep the payment with the client's agreement. Option C is wrong in stating that the solicitor must return the payment – the money will either go to the client or remain with the solicitor, depending on whether or not the client agrees that the solicitor can keep the money.

However, there is no requirement to actually pay it to the client. The solicitor can keep the payment with the client's consent. Option E therefore is not the best answer.

6 Confidentiality

SQE1 syllabus

This chapter will help you to achieve the SQE1 Assessment Specification in relation to Functioning Legal Knowledge concerned with Ethics and Professional Conduct on:

- the purpose, scope and content of the SRA Principles,
- the purpose, scope and content of the SRA Code of Conduct for Solicitors, RELs and RFLs.

Ethics and Professional Conduct is a pervasive topic in SQE1 and may be examined across all subject areas.

Note that for SQE1, candidates are not usually required to recall specific case names or cite statutory or regulatory authorities. Cases are provided for illustrative purposes only.

Learning outcomes

By the end of this chapter you will be able to demonstrate your ability to act honestly and with integrity, and in accordance with the SRA Standards and Regulations in relation to:

- confidentiality and disclosure.

6.1 Introduction

Confidentiality is a fundamental principle of the solicitor–client relationship. For example, it is important that a solicitor receives all the relevant information from a client in order to give the best possible advice. A client would be dissuaded from informing their solicitor of all the relevant facts if the client thought that this information would be released to the public.

This chapter looks at:

- the requirement of confidentiality
- duty of disclosure
- placing confidential information at risk
- confidentiality and privilege.

6.2 The requirement of confidentiality

By the very nature of their work solicitors are privy to all manner of information about their clients. That information could be personal in nature or commercially sensitive; alternatively, it could be totally routine and mundane. Whatever the nature of the information, the client is entitled to expect that it will be kept confidential.

6.2.1 The duty

Paragraph 6.3 provides:

> You [must] keep the affairs of current and former clients confidential unless disclosure is required or permitted by law or the client consents.

The requirement to keep confidentiality prevents the solicitor from communicating the information, and also extends to preventing the use or misuse of information.

The duty of confidentiality applies to all information about a client or matter, regardless of the source of that information. Confidentiality attaches to all information provided by the client or a third party in connection with the retainer. Despite the wide ambit of the duty, there will be no duty of confidentiality where the solicitor is being used by the client to perpetrate fraud or another a crime.

The duty of confidentiality is owed to former, as well as existing, clients and it therefore continues after the retainer has been terminated. The duty also continues after the death of the client, whereupon the right to enforce or waive the duty of confidentiality is passed to the client's (or former client's) personal representatives.

Paragraph 6.3 is replicated in the SRA Code of Conduct for Firms. All members of a firm, including support staff, owe a duty of confidentiality to clients of the firm. Firms must have in place effective systems to enable risks to client confidentiality to be identified and managed.

Any breach of the duty of confidentiality will be a breach of professional conduct. The solicitor may be disciplined by the SRA, or by the Solicitors Disciplinary Tribunal. In addition, the client (or former client) may sue the solicitor for any breach of this duty.

6.2.2 Client consent

Information which would ordinarily be confidential can be disclosed with the client's consent. A solicitor should only seek such consent when the disclosure is necessary, and in the client's best interests. The solicitor must ensure that the client understands exactly what information will be disclosed, when and to whom, and the purpose of the disclosure.

6.2.3 Required or permitted by law

A solicitor may also disclose confidential information when disclosure is required or permitted by law. Examples of circumstances requiring or permitting disclosure are:

(a) pursuant to a statutory requirement, eg to His Majesty's Revenue and Customs in certain circumstances;

(b) pursuant to a statutory duty, such as in the Proceeds of Crime Act 2002 and the Money Laundering, Terrorist Financing and Transfer of Funds (Information on the Payer) Regulations 2017 (SI 2017/692) and under the anti-terrorism legislation (see **Legal Services**);

(c) under a court order, or where a police warrant permits the seizure of confidential documentation;

(d) in some circumstances where a solicitor is acting for a client under a power of attorney or as a court appointed deputy;

(e) in compliance with a notice served by the Legal Ombudsman under s 147 of the Legal Services Act 2007 requiring the production of information/documentation to facilitate the investigation of a complaint.

6.2.4 Circumstances which may justify disclosure

In its Guidance: Confidentiality of Client Information, the SRA gives examples of circumstances which, although still technically amounting to a breach of the duty of confidentiality, may be taken into account as mitigation in the context of disciplinary action. It should be noted that none of them allows for disclosure after the event.

The examples set out in the Guidance are as follows:

(a) *Where a client has indicated their intention to commit suicide or serious self-harm.* The SRA advises that, in the first instance, the solicitor should consider seeking consent from the client to disclose that information to a third party but, where this is not possible or appropriate, the solicitor may decide to disclose the information to the relevant person or authority without consent in order to protect the client or another person.

(b) *Preventing harm to children or vulnerable adults.* This covers situations where the child or adult indicates that they are suffering sexual or other abuse, or where the client discloses abuse either by themselves or by another adult against a child or vulnerable adult. Whilst there is no requirement in law to disclose this information, the solicitor may consider that the threat to the person's life or health is sufficiently serious to justify a breach of the duty of confidentiality.

(c) *Preventing the commission of a criminal offence.* At common law, if a solicitor is being used by a client to perpetrate a fraud or any other crime, the duty of confidentiality does not arise. In other circumstances, a breach may be mitigated where disclosure is made to the extent that the solicitor believes it necessary to prevent the client or a third party from committing a criminal act that the solicitor believes, on reasonable grounds, is likely to result in serious bodily harm.

6.3 Duty of disclosure

When acting for a client on a matter, a solicitor must make the client aware of all information material to the matter of which the solicitor has knowledge (Paragraph 6.4). This is a personal duty, and so the knowledge of the information in question must be that of the individual solicitor, rather than the information being known within the firm as a whole or within the knowledge of another individual in the firm.

The requirement to disclose all information material to the client's matter of which the solicitor is personally aware is subject to a number of exceptions:

(a) the disclosure of the information is prohibited by legal restrictions imposed in the interests of national security or the prevention of crime;

(b) the client gives informed consent, given or evidenced in writing, to the information not being disclosed to them;

(c) the solicitor has reason to believe that serious physical or mental injury will be caused to the client or another if the information is disclosed to the client; or

(d) the information is contained in a privileged document that the solicitor has knowledge of only because it has been mistakenly disclosed.

The last of these exceptions takes account of the fact that due to the volume of information which passes between solicitors on a daily basis, occasionally mistakes may be made and information destined for a third party may be inadvertently disclosed to a solicitor. For example, a solicitor acting for one party in a matter may misaddress correspondence destined for their client to the solicitor acting for the other party. In this case, immediately on becoming aware of the error, the receiving solicitor must return the papers to the originating solicitor without reading them or otherwise making use of the information contained therein (*Ablitt v Mills & Reeve* (1995) *The Times*, 25 October). The exception means that a solicitor is not under a duty to disclose to the client details of any material received in such circumstances.

6.4 Placing confidential information at risk

A solicitor must act in the best interests of the client (Principle 7) and so must not place themselves in a situation where any relevant information could be disclosed to another client, as any such disclosure would be against the best interests of the client to whom the solicitor owes a duty of confidentiality. In order to protect against any accidental disclosure, the Code of Conduct for Solicitors provides that a solicitor must not act in certain circumstances.

6.4.1 The general prohibition

Paragraph 6.5 provides that a solicitor must not act for a client in a matter where that client has an interest adverse to the interest of another current or former client for whom confidential information which is material to that matter is held unless either of the exceptions set out in the Code is met.

6.4.1.1 Material information

For the purposes of the prohibition in Paragraph 6.5, the confidential information held by the solicitor must be 'material'. This term is not further explained in the Code of Conduct for Solicitors, but is likely to encompass information which is relevant to the client's matter and of more than inconsequential interest to the client.

The question of whether the information is 'material' relates to the client to whom the duty of disclosure concerning the information is owed.

6.4.1.2 Adverse interest

For the purposes of the prohibition in Paragraph 6.5 there must be adverse interests. Adversity relates to the relationship between the two respective clients, namely the client for whom the solicitor is considering acting and a current or former client for whom the solicitor holds confidential information.

The relationship can be said to be adverse where the client to whom the solicitor owes the duty of confidentiality is, or is likely to become, an opposing party in a matter to the client who is owed the duty of disclosure. This would include a situation where the clients litigate against each other, are involved in mediation, or even if the clients are on opposing sides of a negotiation. However, there is an argument for saying that the concept of an adverse interest should be interpreted in a wider sense, that is, in relation to a particular matter, whether the one client would want to receive the information because it is potentially of value to them, and whether the other client would want that information to remain confidential.

6.4.2 The exceptions

Paragraph 6.5 provides that it would be possible to act for a client in a matter where that client has an interest adverse to the interest of another current or former client for whom confidential information is held which is material to that matter if either of the following exceptions are met:

- effective measures have been taken which result in there being no real risk of disclosure of the confidential information; or

- the current or former client whose information is held has given informed consent, given or evidenced in writing, to the solicitor acting, including to any measures taken to protect their information.

In practice, it is more likely that these exceptions will apply where the client to whom the duty of confidentiality is owed is a former client.

6.4.2.1 Effective measures

The measures must protect one client's confidential information from the other client and their solicitor. Whilst there can be no absolute guarantees, in order to be considered effective the measures must be such as to result in there being 'no real risk' of confidential information being accidentally or inadvertently disclosed. Accordingly, the bar is set high.

From a practical point of view, it will be difficult for an individual solicitor to put protective measures in place. This exception is more likely to be relevant at a firm level taking steps to prevent confidential information, given by a client to one part of a firm, from being made available to another part of the same firm (Paragraph 6.5 is replicated in the SRA Code of Conduct for Firms). Effective measures would include information barriers, which are practical steps taken to ensure that confidential information cannot pass from one client to another client. Practical arrangements such as physical separation within the building of those acting for each client, information being encrypted and password protected and separate servers may protect information in larger firms; this may not be appropriate for smaller firms.

6.4.2.2 Informed consent

To come within this exception, in broad terms, the client(s) must consent after having understood and considered the risks and rewards involved in the situation. The onus is on the solicitor to ensure that the client understands the issues. One of the difficulties with seeking such consent is that it is often not possible to disclose sufficient information about the identity and business of the other client without breaching that other client's confidentiality. It would be for the solicitor to decide in each case whether it would be able to provide sufficient information for the client to be able to give 'informed consent'.

'Informed consent' is more likely to be appropriate for 'sophisticated clients', such as large companies with in-house legal advisers or other expertise, who would be able to assess the risks of giving their consent based on the information provided.

6.4.3 Confidentiality vs disclosure

There will be circumstances in which a solicitor's duty of confidentiality conflicts with their duty to disclose. Typically, this will arise when a solicitor holds confidential information for a former client which the solicitor would ordinarily be obliged to disclose to a new client.

⭐ *Example*

> *Jacob, a solicitor, is instructed by Sam in the purchase of a derelict plot of land from Lycen Ltd. Sam intends to build a new house on the land. One of Jacob's former clients, Amy, sold the land to Lycen Ltd two years ago at a knock-down price having revealed to Jacob that the land is contaminated. This information would be material to Sam's matter as information concerning the state of the land is relevant to whether Sam will want to buy it. However, the two clients are not instructing the firm in relation to the same matter and so, on a strict interpretation, their interests are not adverse to one another and consequently the prohibition in Paragraph 6.5 does not apply. However, Jacob could not inform Sam of the contamination because his duty of confidentiality to Amy would remain.*

In such circumstances the solicitor could not act in the best interests of the new client without breaching their duty of confidentiality to the former client. In its Guidance: Unregulated Organisations – Conflict and Confidentiality, the SRA says that the fact that a solicitor cannot meet their obligations to the new client because of their obligation to the former client will be no defence to a breach of Paragraph 6.4. Consequently, the Guidance is that the solicitor must not act for the new client in the absence of informed consent from the new client to the information not being disclosed to them. By analogy the same principle should apply to solicitors generally given the need to act in the client's best interests.

One situation in which the duties of confidentiality and disclosure may conflict is where a solicitor is acting for both the borrower and lender on a mortgage taken out to fund a purchase in a residential conveyancing transaction (see also **7.6.3**) and there is a suggestion of mortgage fraud. Mortgage fraud may be committed in many ways; for example, the borrower overstating their income in order to obtain a higher mortgage or one joint buyer forging the other's signature (see also **4.2.2** on the risk of fraud). A problem will arise if the solicitor has any information about the transaction that the lender would consider relevant to granting the loan, but the borrower does not want the solicitor to disclose it to the lender. There is an obligation to disclose all relevant information to the lender client, but the solicitor also has a duty of confidentiality to the borrower client. Accordingly, the solicitor must seek consent from the borrower to disclose the information to the lender, but if that consent is not given the solicitor must refuse to continue to act for the borrower and the lender. (The solicitor may also have obligations under the Proceeds of Crime Act 2002 (see **Legal Services**).) Although, if there is a strong prima facie case that the borrower is using the solicitor to further a fraud or other criminal purpose, the solicitor will cease to owe a duty of confidentiality in any event (see **6.2.1**).

6.4.4 Overlap with conflict of interests

Where a solicitor holds confidential information for one current client which is relevant to another current client in the same or a related matter, that particular solicitor will be unable to act for both clients unless the client to whom the duty of confidentiality is owed consents to the information being disclosed or the other client gives informed consent, given or evidenced in writing, to the information not being disclosed to them. In the absence of such consents, the solicitor owes a personal duty of disclosure to one client whilst owing a duty of confidentiality to the other and so a conflict of interests arises (see **Chapter 7**). Consequently, the existence of a conflict of interest may prevent a solicitor from acting, irrespective of the exceptions in Paragraph 6.5.

6.4.5 Professional embarrassment

Even where the general prohibition in Paragraph 6.5 does not apply or one of the exceptions can be relied upon, thus allowing a solicitor or a firm to act for two clients, a solicitor might still be obliged to refuse to act on the grounds of professional embarrassment. A solicitor should decline to act where the information which cannot be disclosed to the client would cause severe embarrassment if the fact that the solicitor had agreed to act in those circumstances ever came out.

A solicitor should also consider the Principles, such as whether the solicitor will be able to act in the best interests of the client in question, and public trust in the legal profession.

6.5   Confidentiality and privilege

The obligation of confidentiality is distinct from the issue of legal professional privilege. Whilst confidentiality prevents a solicitor from disclosing any information relating to a client, legal professional privilege allows a solicitor to withhold specific information which the solicitor would otherwise be required to disclose, for example in court proceedings. Privilege can only be waived by the client.

Legal professional privilege applies to information which is passed between a solicitor and a client, whether written or oral, directly or indirectly. The rationale behind this right to withhold information, even from the court, is similar to the rationale for the obligation of confidentiality – it exists to enable a client to speak to the solicitor without worrying that the information passed over might be disclosed at a later date. However, there are limitations in place to prevent legal professional privilege being used as a cloak to hide information which a client does not wish a court to see.

Legal advice privilege applies only to information passed between the client and a solicitor *acting in the capacity of a solicitor*. In other words, the communication must relate to the request for, or the provision of, advice to the client by the solicitor. If documents are sent to or from an independent third party, even if they are created for the purpose of obtaining legal advice, they will not be covered by this privilege, and therefore simply 'copying in' a solicitor will not mean the information can be withheld. If the communication is made for the purpose of committing a fraud or a crime, it will not attract privilege (*R v Cox and Railton* (1884) LR 14 QBD 153).

Clients and solicitors may also claim litigation privilege in respect of documents created for the sole or dominant purpose of litigation or other adversarial proceedings which have already commenced or are contemplated. This privilege also extends to communications between a solicitor and third parties. A related issue which also arises in the case of litigation is that anything said by a solicitor whilst speaking in court as an advocate is privileged. Therefore the solicitor cannot be sued for defamation in such circumstances.

Like the duty of confidentiality, privilege continues beyond the death of a client (*Bullivant v A-G for Victoria* [1901] AC 196).

The UK General Data Protection Regulation (GDPR) and the Data Protection Act 2018 impose a high level of transparency on firms in the context of informing clients and other individuals if it is processing their personal data and providing a copy of that data if they request it (by a 'subject access request'). The Data Protection Act 2018 contains an exception to these requirements in Sch 2 for information in respect of which a claim to legal professional privilege could be maintained in legal proceedings or in respect of which the duty of confidentiality is owed to a client by a professional legal adviser. As a result, data subjects' rights under the data protection regime do not take precedence over legal professional privilege or client confidentiality when it comes to transparency.

Summary

- A solicitor must keep the affairs of their clients confidential.
- The duty of confidentiality continues until the client permits disclosure or waives the confidentiality.
- The duty of confidentiality may be overridden in exceptional circumstances.

- The solicitor also has a personal duty to disclose to the client all information that is relevant to the client's matter.

- A solicitor must not risk breaching confidentiality by acting for a client where that client has an interest adverse to the interest of another current or former client for whom the solicitor holds confidential information which is material to that matter, unless appropriate safeguards can be put in place to prevent disclosure of the confidential information or the client to whom the duty of confidentiality is owed gives informed consent to the solicitor acting.

- Where legal professional privilege applies, a solicitor can refuse to disclose communications between himself and a client.

Sample questions

Question 1

A solicitor is acting for the claimant in a contract dispute. Shortly before the final hearing, the defendant's brief to counsel in the case is delivered to the solicitor's office by mistake.

What should the solicitor do?

A   Read the brief and then make the client aware of any of the contents which are material to the client's matter.

B   Immediately return the brief to the defendant's solicitors without reading it.

C   Read the brief and then make use of its contents at the final hearing.

D   Ask the client for instructions on whether to return the brief.

E   Destroy the brief without reading it.

Answer

Option B is correct. Where a solicitor receives confidential information by mistake, immediately on becoming aware of the error, the solicitor must return the papers to the originating solicitor without reading them or otherwise making use of their contents (*Ablitt v Mills & Reeve* [1995]). Paragraph 6.4 (d) provides for an express exception to the duty to disclose information material to a client's matter when such information is mistakenly disclosed via a privileged document.

Question 2

A solicitor drew up a will for a client. The terms of the will appointed the client's widow as executor and left the entire estate to the client's son. The client died last week. The client's son contacts the solicitor and explains that he is in debt and that he urgently needs proof that he will soon receive an inheritance to show to his main creditor otherwise the creditor will start bankruptcy proceedings against him. The son requests a copy of the will.

Which of the following best explains how the solicitor should respond to the request?

A   Immediately email a copy of the will to the son because this is in the client's best interests.

B   Immediately email a copy of the will to the son because the solicitor's duty of confidentiality ceased on the client's death.

C   Offer to immediately write a letter to the creditor confirming that the entire estate will pass to the son because the duty of confidentiality only arises in respect of a copy of the will itself.

D   Ask the widow for consent to release a copy of the will because the duty of confidentiality has passed to the widow.

E   Immediately email a copy of the will to the son because the need to avoid bankruptcy proceedings is an example of the disclosure of confidential information being required by law.

Answer

Option D is correct. The duty of confidentiality in Paragraph 6.3 extends to current and former clients and survives death of a client. On death the duty of confidentiality passes to the personal representatives. Accordingly, the solicitor cannot provide a copy of the will in the absence of consent from the widow as executor, and options A and B are therefore wrong. (Once the Will is proved it will become a public document but in the interim the solicitor must maintain confidentiality.) The content of the will, not just a copy of it, is confidential (with the result that option C is wrong). Option E is wrong – there is no legal requirement on the facts necessitating disclosure of confidential information.

Question 3

A solicitor is instructed by a new client in the purchase of a house. One of the solicitor's former clients sold the house to its current owner 12 months ago at a much reduced price because the house had been flooded twice in the previous three years. The new client does not know that the house is at risk of flooding.

Which of the following best describes the position with regard to the solicitor's duty of disclosure?

A   The solicitor can only disclose the risk of flooding to the new client with the former client's consent.

B   The solicitor must disclose the risk of flooding to the new client because the duty of disclosure takes precedence over the duty of confidentiality.

C   The solicitor has no duty to disclose the risk of flooding to the new client because the information is not material to the retainer.

D   The solicitor can disclose the risk of flooding to the new client because the solicitor owes no duty of confidentiality to the former client following termination of the retainer.

E   The solicitor must disclose the risk of flooding to the new client because this is in the new client's best interests.

Answer

Option A is correct. The solicitor owes a duty of confidentiality to the former client; option D therefore is wrong. Option E is wrong as the duty of confidentiality can only be overridden with the former client's consent (note that disclosure is not required or permitted by law on these facts). The duty of disclosure does not take precedence; option B is wrong. Option C is wrong as the risk of flooding will have an effect on price and insurability which will affect whether the new client wants to buy the property and so the information is material to the retainer.

7 Conflicts

SQE1 syllabus

This chapter will help you to achieve the SQE1 Assessment Specification in relation to Functioning Legal Knowledge concerned with Ethics and Professional Conduct on:

- the purpose, scope and content of the SRA Principles,
- the purpose, scope and content of the SRA Code of Conduct for Solicitor, RELs and RFLs.

Ethics and Professional Conduct is a pervasive topic in SQE1 and may be examined across all subject areas.

Note that for SQE1, candidates are not usually required to recall specific case names or cite statutory or regulatory authorities.

Learning outcomes

By the end of this chapter you will be able to demonstrate your ability to act honestly and with integrity, and in accordance with the SRA Standards and Regulations in relation to:

- conflict of interest.

7.1 Introduction

A solicitor must act in the best interests of the client (Principle 7). There will be situations where the interests of two clients (or prospective clients) conflict. Where this happens, it will be practically impossible for the solicitor to act in the best interests of the two clients simultaneously. There may also be circumstances in which the interests of the client conflict with the solicitor's own personal interests so that it would be impossible for the solicitor to give objective and unbiased advice.

The SRA prohibits solicitors from acting where such conflicts arise, except in specified limited circumstances.

This chapter looks at:

- types of conflict of interests
- conflict of interest between clients
- own interest conflict
- limited retainer
- property transactions.

7.2 Types of conflict of interests

Paragraphs 6.1 and 6.2 provide that there are two situations where a conflict of interests may arise:

(a) a conflict between the client's interests and the solicitor's interests (an 'own interest conflict'); or

(b) a conflict between two or more clients (a 'conflict of interest').

A solicitor can never act where there is a conflict between the solicitor's own interests and the interests of a current client.

There are limited circumstances in which a solicitor can act where there is a conflict between two or more current clients. Even in these circumstances, however, the overriding consideration will be the best interests of each of the clients concerned, and in particular whether the solicitor is satisfied that it is reasonable to act for all or both the clients.

Paragraphs 6.1 and 6.2 are repeated in the SRA Code of Conduct for Firms. This would, for example, prevent one solicitor within the firm acting for a client whose interests are in conflict with those of the client of another solicitor within the same firm.

7.3 Conflict of interest between clients

For the purposes of the Code of Conduct, a conflict of interest means 'a situation where the solicitor's or firm's separate duties to act in the best interests of two or more clients conflict' (SRA Glossary).

Paragraph 6.2 provides that a solicitor or firm must not act in relation to a matter or particular aspect of it if there is a conflict of interest or a significant risk of such a conflict in relation to that matter or aspect of it, unless:

(a) the clients have a substantially common interest in relation to the matter or the aspect of it, as appropriate; or

(b) the clients are competing for the same objective.

7.3.1 Current clients

A conflict of interest may arise only between two or more current clients. Where a client's retainer has been terminated the solicitor no longer owes a duty to act in that client's best interests, and so a conflict of interest cannot arise concerning the affairs of a former client. However, the solicitor must still bear in mind the duty of confidentiality owed to former clients (see **Chapter 6**).

A solicitor should decline to act at the outset in order to ensure that a conflict of interest does not arise in the first place, rather than start to act and risk a conflict arising at a later date. However, a situation may arise where a solicitor has agreed to act for two clients when, at the beginning of the transaction, there was genuinely no actual conflict or any significant risk of a conflict apparent on the facts, but a conflict then arises during the retainer. In these circumstances, the solicitor cannot continue to act for both clients. Whether the solicitor is able to continue for act for one client will depend on the solicitor being able to maintain client confidentiality (see **Chapter 6**).

7.3.2 'The same matter or a particular aspect of it'

It is easy to see how a conflict of interest might arise when advising two clients about the same matter.

⭐ *Example*

> *Omi is a solicitor. Omi is asked to act for Mr Lacey and Mr Roberts, who are suing each other over a boundary dispute. Both clients will ultimately want to win their case, and so Omi will have a duty to act in the best interests of each client and take steps to try to ensure that they are successful in their litigation. However, Omi would be placed in an impossible situation, as anything done to help Mr Lacey win his case will be detrimental to Mr Roberts' case (and therefore not in Mr Roberts' best interests).*

Acting for clients whose interests are in direct conflict, for example claimant and defendant in litigation, will almost inevitably result in a conflict of interest, making it impossible to act for both parties. Likewise, acting for two or more clients where the solicitor may need to negotiate on matters of substance on their behalf, for example negotiating on price between a seller and a purchaser, is also likely to result in a conflict of interest as separate duties will be owed to each client to act in their best interests and those duties conflict or there is a significant risk that they will do so. Whilst these are examples of situations in which there would normally be a clear conflict of interest preventing the solicitor from acting, it is for the solicitor to decide whether or not a conflict in fact arises in the particular circumstances of the case.

A conflict of interest can also arise concerning a particular aspect of a matter rather than the matter as a whole. For example, a solicitor could not act to sell a new house for one client whilst also acting for another client who is alleging that a part of the house has been built on his land.

Where the only conflict between the parties is their wider business interests then this will not create any conflict of interest issues.

⭐ *Example*

> *Isla Cola and Samet Cola are the two main cola distributors in England and Wales. James, a solicitor, is asked to represent Isla Cola on a purchase of a new IT system for their factory. James is already representing Samet Cola in the purchase of a fleet of cars for their management.*
>
> *The business interests of Isla Cola and Samet Cola will conflict in that they will both want to sell more cola than the other firm. However, James can act for both at the same time without breaching the Code as the purchases of the IT system and the cars are not the same matter.*

7.3.3 Significant risk of a conflict of interest

It is not necessary for there to be an actual conflict of interest. A significant risk that a solicitor's duties to act in the best interests of each client may conflict will be enough to bring it within Paragraph 6.2.

⭐ *Example*

> *Loreta, a solicitor, is approached by Temi and Demitrij, who are partners in a firm of surveyors. Temi explains that she wishes to leave the partnership and that Demitrij has agreed to buy her interest in the partnership. Temi and Demitrij say that as they have agreed on the price they do not wish to go to the expense of instructing different solicitors to act for them.*
>
> *Can Loreta act for both of them in agreeing the sale of Temi's interest in the partnership?*
>
> *On the face of it, the parties are in agreement and at present there may be no actual conflict between them. However, there is a significant risk of such a conflict arising: Temi might want to increase the price once Loreta has given advice about her legal rights, and Demitrij might not agree; there will be other significant terms to be negotiated such as liability for the firm's debts. In the circumstances Loreta cannot act for both clients.*

Each case must be judged on its individual circumstances. A solicitor can act if, on the facts, there is no significant risk of a conflict arising.

7.3.4 Exceptions

Where a conflict of interest exists, or where there is a significant risk that a conflict may exist, a solicitor may still act for both parties in defined circumstances and with the informed consent of both parties.

7.3.4.1 The substantially common interest exception

Where there is a conflict of interest or a significant risk of one, a solicitor can still act where the clients have a substantially common interest in relation to the matter or the aspect of it, as appropriate (Paragraph 6.2(a)).

The SRA Glossary defines 'a substantially common interest' as a situation where there is a clear common purpose between the clients and a strong consensus as to how it is to be achieved.

An example of when this exception might be used is where a solicitor is instructed by a group of people who want to set up a company. Whilst those providing instructions may not necessarily agree on every aspect involved in setting up a new business venture, so long as they have agreed upon the key, fundamental matters (such as funding, shareholdings, management structure and roles etc), it is likely that a clear common purpose and a strong consensus as to how this will be achieved can be said to exist and so enable the solicitor to act for the group in setting up the company. However, if differences were to arise within the group during the course of the matter which could be seen as undermining the common purpose and strong consensus, the solicitor is likely to come to the conclusion that the exception no longer applies and so would have to cease to act for the group as a conflict of interest has arisen.

7.3.4.2 The competing for the same objective (or 'commercial') exception

Where there is a conflict of interest or a significant risk of one, a solicitor can still act where the clients are competing for the same objective (Paragraph 6.2(b)).

The SRA Glossary sets out the meaning of some of the terminology used in this exception to aid in its interpretation. Clients will be 'competing for the same objective' in a situation in which two or more clients are competing for an 'objective' which, if attained by one client, will make that 'objective' unattainable to the other client or clients. The term 'objective' is further defined as an asset, contract or business opportunity which two or more clients are seeking to acquire or recover through liquidation (or some other form of insolvency process) or by means of an auction or tender process or a bid or offer, but not a public takeover.

This exception is likely, therefore, to be used for corporate clients only. For example, it would enable one firm to act for two companies bidding to take over a third company, despite the fact that the obligations to act in the best interests of the clients would conflict (both want to be successful in their bid to acquire the company, and any step taken by the firm to try to make this happen for one client would be detrimental to the interests of the other client).

7.3.4.3 Conditions for acting

A set of conditions must be met if a solicitor is to be able to act for two or more clients under either of the exceptions in Paragraph 6.2:

(a) all the clients have given informed consent, given or evidenced in writing, to the solicitor acting;

(b) where appropriate, effective safeguards are put in place to protect the clients' confidential information; and

(c) the solicitor is satisfied it is reasonable to act for all the clients.

Informed consent

A client simply agreeing to the solicitor acting will not be enough. The consent must be 'informed', meaning that the client must appreciate the issues and risks involved (having had these explained by the solicitor, where appropriate) and make a decision based on those risks. Informed consent may be easier to obtain from sophisticated users of legal services, such as large companies with in-house legal departments to advise them on the risks involved of being represented under one of the exceptions.

Confidential information

Where a solicitor does decide to act by taking advantage of one of the above exceptions, it may be that confidential information is held for one client which is material to the other client(s). Where this is the case, effective safeguards must be put in place to protect the confidential information. It may be difficult for an individual solicitor to achieve this, but a firm may be able to do so in order to enable separate solicitors within the same firm to act.

Reasonable to act

When considering whether to use one of the above exceptions it must also be reasonable for the solicitor to act for all the clients. The solicitor should consider – both at the outset and throughout the duration of the retainer – whether one client is at risk of prejudice if not represented separately (ie by another firm) from the other client(s). This will particularly be the case where one client is vulnerable, the clients cannot be represented even-handedly or where the parties do not have equal bargaining power.

7.4 Own interest conflict

Paragraph 6.1 provides that a solicitor must not act where there is an 'own interest' conflict, or a significant risk of an 'own interest' conflict. This refers to any situation where a solicitor's duty to act in the best interests of any client in relation to a matter conflicts, or there is a significant risk that it may conflict, with the solicitor's own interests in relation to that or a related matter (SRA Glossary). In such a situation, the solicitor or the firm must consider whether to decline to accept the retainer, cease to act where instructions have already been accepted or advise the client to seek independent legal advice on that aspect of the matter.

For example, a solicitor could not act for a client suing a company where the solicitor was a major shareholder in that company. The solicitor would be obliged to act in the best interests of the client and take steps to try to ensure that the client was successful in suing the company. In taking those steps the solicitor would be acting to the detriment of the company. If the client was successful, the company would have to pay the client damages and so its share price might drop. This would be detrimental to the company's shareholders – including the solicitor.

There are no exceptions to Paragraph 6.1. So, for example, the solicitor cannot act even though the client consents to the solicitor acting.

SRA Guidance: Conflict of Interests includes the following examples of situations in which a solicitor's interest might conflict with that of a client:

(a) A financial interest of yours or someone close to you. For example, a client asks you to carry out due diligence on a company which you or your spouse/partner own shares in.

(b) A personal or business relationship of yours. For example, where you are asked to advise on a claim against a relative of yours, a friend or someone with whom you are involved with in a common financial enterprise.

(c) Your role as an employee. For example, a client asks for advice in relation to a dispute involving your employer or a fellow employee.

(d) Your own conduct (as a firm or an individual). For example, the wrong advice has been given to the client or the wrong action taken on their behalf.

One situation which could give rise to an own interest in conflict is where a solicitor is asked to draft a will in which the client wishes to make a gift of significant value to the solicitor or a member of the solicitor's family, or an employee of the solicitor's business or their family. 'Significant' in this context includes a gift which is either significant in itself or in relation to the size of the estate. In its Guidance: Drafting and Preparation of Wills the SRA makes it clear that each case must be judged on its merits, but usually the effect of Paragraph 6.1 will be to prevent the solicitor acting unless the client agrees to take independent legal advice on making the gift (see also **4.3.3**).

An own interest conflict may occur where something has gone wrong in the client's case or the solicitor has made a mistake. In such a situation Paragraph 7.11 requires the solicitor to be open and honest with the client. In some cases, all that will be required is for the solicitor to tell the client what has happened and then, with the client's agreement, take the appropriate remedial action. However, there will be cases which give rise to an own interest conflict or a risk of such a conflict, for example where one of the client's options is to bring a claim for negligence against the solicitor. In such cases, the client must be told to seek independent legal advice (see also **1.9**).

7.5 Limited retainer

Where a conflict arises between two clients, either at the beginning of or during a transaction, an alternative to relying on one of the exceptions in Paragraph 6.2 may be to accept a limited retainer. The solicitor could be retained to act only in relation to those areas where no conflict exists, with each client seeking independent advice on the conflicting areas. It is necessary to make clear the terms of the retainer, and that there are defined areas where the solicitor cannot advise.

7.6 Property transactions

Dealing with property transactions, particularly in the residential sector, is one area of practice which has the potential for giving rise to a conflict of interest.

7.6.1 Acting for buyer and seller

Sometimes a solicitor is asked to act for both buyer and seller in a property transaction. Typically this happens when both parties are existing clients of the solicitor's firm on other matters or where the parties feel that, as they have already reached an agreement through the estate agent, they can save time and costs by having the same solicitor deal with the paperwork.

SRA Guidance: Conflict of Interests gives one client selling or leasing an asset to another client as an example of a situation that can give rise to a conflict of interest and states that a solicitor should not normally act for two or more clients in these circumstances. The potential for a conflict arising is obvious. For example, there may be substantial terms still to be negotiated or an adverse survey may require the purchase price to be renegotiated. However, the SRA does not specifically prohibit a solicitor acting for both buyer and seller.

It is therefore for the solicitor to decide on the individual facts of the case whether there is a conflict of interest or a significant risk of one arising. The solicitor will need to consider all the facts. The nature of the transaction may be significant; for example, in high-value or complex transactions, there is a greater likelihood of substantial negotiations, increasing the risk of a conflict. The nature of parties may be significant; for example, vulnerability or an inequality of bargaining power makes it more difficult to act in the best interests of both clients.

If there is a conflict of interest the solicitor is highly unlikely to come within either exception in Paragraph 6.2. Buyer and seller are not competing for the same asset and therefore do not satisfy the definition of 'competing for the same objective'. It may be for the solicitor to determine whether buyer and seller can be said to have a substantially common interest. There is no specific provision in the SRA Codes of Conduct, but historically the SRA's view has been that a buyer and seller do not have a substantially common interest and recent advice from the Law Society confirms that this is the case.

Although there is no ban on a solicitor acting for buyer and seller, the circumstances in which a solicitor will be able to conclude that there is no conflict of interests, or significant risk of one occurring, will be rare. However, it might be possible to act, for example, where the property is being transferred between family members or where the parties are associated companies.

7.6.2 Acting for joint buyers

It is common practice for one solicitor to act for joint buyers of a property. It will usually be the case that the interests of both buyers are the same and therefore no conflict arises. However, the solicitor must assess each case on its merits and recognise those cases which are outside the norm, for example where one buyer is being forced or pressurised into the transaction by the other.

7.6.3 Acting for borrower and lender

Many buyers will fund the purchase price with the aid of a loan or mortgage. In a commercial property context it is common for buyer and lender to be separately represented, but in a residential transaction the buyer's solicitor will often be asked to act for the lender as well. Whatever the context, the solicitor will need to decide whether a conflict of interest arises (see also **6.4.4**).

The circumstances in which a conflict could arise include where the terms of the mortgage offer are unfair to the borrower, the buyer is unable to comply with the mortgage terms or substantial negotiation will be required.

In residential transactions, the borrower will often be borrowing from a high street bank or building society where the mortgage is offered on standard terms and conditions with no negotiation being necessary. It may be possible to conclude that no conflict of interests arises in such circumstances or, if there is, that there is a 'substantially common interest' in that both the borrower and the lender want a good and marketable title to the property to be acquired.

Summary

- a solicitor must not act where there is a conflict, or significant risk of a conflict, between the interests of two or more clients, or between the interests of the client and the solicitor;

- where there is a conflict between two or more clients, a solicitor may act if the solicitor can satisfy the requirements of the substantially common interest exception or the competing for the same objective exception.

Sample questions

Question 1

A solicitor is asked to act in a boundary dispute. The prospective client owns a piece of land adjacent to a company's warehouse premises. The company has recently erected a fence which encroaches onto the land. The solicitor tells the prospective client that the solicitor is on the company's board of directors. However, the solicitor reassures the prospective client that the solicitor does not act for the company and that the solicitor will keep the prospective client's information confidential.

Is the solicitor able to act for the prospective client?

A   Yes, because the prospective client is aware of the solicitor's directorship.

B   Yes, because effective safeguards are in place to protect the prospective client's confidential information.

C   Yes, because there is no connection between the directorship and the solicitor's professional work.

D   No, because there is an own interest conflict.

E   No, because there is a conflict of interest between the prospective client and the company.

Answer

Option D is correct. This is an own interest conflict and therefore the solicitor cannot act in any circumstances (Paragraph 6.1). There are no exceptions contained in Paragraph 6.1. The company is not a client and so there can be no conflict of interest.

Question 2

A father is selling one of his many properties to his daughter at a substantial undervalue to help her to get a start on the property ladder. They both ask the same solicitor to carry out the conveyancing work for them.

Which of the following best explains who the solicitor can act for?

A   The solicitor cannot act for either as there is a conflict of interest between father and daughter.

B   The solicitor cannot act for either as there is an own interest conflict.

C   The solicitor can act for both as they are 'competing for the same objective'.

D   The solicitor can act for both as the risk of a conflict of interest is not significant.

E   The solicitor cannot act for the father as selling the property at a substantial undervalue is not in his best interests.

Answer

Option D is correct. Paragraph 6.2 provides that you must not act if there is a client conflict or significant risk of a client conflict. Usually, there will be a client conflict in acting for both seller and buyer in a residential property transaction. However, this will not always be the case. On the facts, this is a case where a conflict is unlikely to arise (option A therefore is not the best answer). The solicitor is not personally involved so there is no own interest conflict (option B is wrong). 'Competing for the same objective' is not involved – they are not in competition to acquire the property (option C is therefore not relevant). Even if a conflict of interest arose it would not prevent the solicitor acting for both parties – the solicitor could act for one. Option E is wrong, as selling the property, even at an undervalue, would achieve the father's objective.

Question 3

A solicitor receives instructions to act for the claimant in a litigation matter. The solicitor's colleague in the firm's litigation department, already acts for the defendant in the same matter.

Can the solicitor act for the claimant?

A   Yes, because the parties have a 'substantially common interest' in the matter.

B   Yes, because the parties are 'competing for the same objective'.

C   Yes, because there is no conflict of interest where the parties are represented by different solicitors within the same firm.

D   No, because there is a conflict of interest.

E   No, because there is an own interest conflict.

Answer

Option D is correct. The clients here have opposite interests as they are on different sides in the dispute. This gives rise to a conflict of interest. Neither exception in Paragraph 6.2 can apply to opponents in litigation, accordingly, options A and B are wrong. Paragraph 6.2 is replicated in the Code for Firms and so applies to the firm as a whole and not just to individual solicitors or employees, meaning that option C is wrong. Option E is wrong as the solicitor has no personal involvement and so there is no own interest conflict.

8 Undertakings

SQE1 syllabus

This chapter will help you to achieve the SQE1 Assessment Specification in relation to Functioning Legal Knowledge concerned with Ethics and Professional Conduct on:

• the purpose, scope and content of the SRA Code of Conduct for Solicitors, RELs and RFLs.

Ethics and Professional Conduct is a pervasive topic in SQE1 and may be examined across all subject areas.

Note that for SQE1, candidates are not usually required to recall specific case names or cite statutory or regulatory authorities. Cases are provided for illustrative purposes only.

Learning outcomes

By the end of this chapter you will be able to demonstrate your ability to act honestly and with integrity, and in accordance with the SRA Standards and Regulations in relation to:

• maintaining trust and acting fairly.

8.1 Introduction

A solicitor must act with integrity (Principle 4). One aspect of acting with integrity is for a solicitor to keep their word. So, if a solicitor makes a promise to do something, the person to whom that promise is made should be able to rely on the solicitor in fact doing so. An undertaking is a type of promise.

This chapter looks at:

- the need for undertakings
- the meaning of undertaking
- breach of an undertaking
- terms of the undertaking
- client's authority
- change of circumstances
- enforcement.

8.2 The need for undertakings

Undertakings are often given by solicitors in order to smooth the path of a transaction. They are a convenient method by which some otherwise problematic areas of practice can be avoided.

⭐ Example

Tariq, a solicitor, is acting for Maria concerning the sale of her business. Maria has agreed that she will pay a fixed sum of £10,000 towards the legal costs of the purchaser. The purchaser wants Maria to pay this money up front before the deal takes place, in order to fund the necessary due diligence process (eg to examine the contracts and leases of the business to establish whether the business is worth the asking price). However, Maria does not have the cash to be able to pay the £10,000 now.

To break the impasse, Tariq could give an undertaking to the purchaser's solicitors to pay £10,000 towards the purchaser's costs from the proceeds of sale of the business. If accepted, the purchaser's solicitors might well be happy to complete the due diligence work without receiving the money now, safe in the knowledge that Tariq will definitely pay the £10,000 to them in due course. By giving the undertaking, Tariq has enabled the sale to proceed.

8.3 The meaning of 'undertaking'

In essence, an undertaking is an enforceable promise. A solicitor will be expected to comply with an undertaking and must therefore ensure that it is honoured. For the purposes of the SRA Standards and Regulations, the SRA Glossary defines an undertaking as:

> a statement given orally or in writing, whether or not it includes the word 'undertake' or 'undertaking' to someone who reasonably places reliance on it, that you or a third party will do something or cause something to be done, or refrain from doing something.

A solicitor must perform all undertakings given by them and do so within an agreed timescale or, if no timescale has been agreed, then within a reasonable amount of time (Paragraph 1.3).

The SRA Glossary definition of an undertaking is quite wide. Any oral or written statement made by a solicitor to do or not do something, whether given to a client or to a third party (such as another solicitor), may be an undertaking. Indeed, even if such a promise is made on a solicitor's behalf by a member of their staff, it may constitute an undertaking. It is not necessary to use the word 'undertake' for the promise to amount to an undertaking. Even a promise to give an undertaking will usually be interpreted as an undertaking, and therefore will be binding on the solicitor concerned.

A solicitor is not obliged to give or accept an undertaking. A solicitor should think carefully when considering whether to give an undertaking. Once the undertaking has been relied upon by the recipient, it can be withdrawn only by agreement.

8.4 Breach of an undertaking

The consequences of breach of an undertaking will depend on the circumstances. The recipient may have a cause of action (eg in contract) enabling them to bring proceedings against the solicitor to enforce it and/or the court may enforce the undertaking summarily (see **8.8.1**). Added to which the solicitor is likely to face some disciplinary action (see **8.8.2**).

Where a solicitor gives an undertaking, the terms of that undertaking will usually be personally binding on the individual solicitor concerned.

✪ Example

Fran, a solicitor, is acting for Marcus who is in arrears with his mortgage payments. Marcus is being taken to court by his mortgage company to repossess his house. To prevent the house being repossessed, Marcus offers to pay the arrears (£10,000) within seven days. The mortgage company agrees to withdraw the repossession proceedings, but only on the basis that Fran gives an undertaking to pay the mortgage company £10,000 within seven days. If Fran agreed to give the undertaking in those terms and Marcus did not come up with the money, Fran would be personally liable to pay the £10,000.

If a solicitor fails to comply with an undertaking, the solicitor may be sued personally by the recipient. The solicitor will also breach the Code of Conduct for Solicitors and may be disciplined by the SRA or the Solicitors Disciplinary Tribunal.

The obligation in Paragraph 1.3 is replicated in the SRA Code of Conduct for Firms. Undertakings given by solicitors, non-admitted staff, and also undertakings given by anyone held out by the firm as representing the firm are binding on the firm. For example, if an undertaking given by an assistant solicitor is not honoured, there will be a breach of professional conduct by the solicitor and also by the partners of the firm.

Solicitors must be able to be able to justify their decisions and actions and demonstrate their compliance with their obligations under the SRA's regulatory arrangements (Paragraph 7.2). A solicitor should therefore maintain an effective system that records when undertakings have been given and when they have been discharged.

8.5 Terms of the undertaking

An undertaking is binding regardless of whether it is given orally or in writing. From the solicitor's point of view, it is advisable to give undertakings in writing, so that there can be no dispute as to the terms of the undertaking. If, however, it is necessary in the circumstances to give an oral undertaking, the solicitor should ensure that an attendance note recording the undertaking is placed on the client's file and that it is confirmed in writing as soon as possible.

An undertaking need not be contractual in nature. For example, there is no obligation for consideration (whether in monetary or other forms) to be present for an undertaking to be enforceable against a solicitor. However, given the binding effect of undertakings, and the consequences for breach, solicitors should take just as much care in drafting undertakings as they would do when drafting a contract for a client. Although not expressly stated in the Code for Solicitors, it is likely that any ambiguity in the wording of the undertaking will be interpreted in favour of its recipient.

✪ Example

Ayesha, a solicitor, is acting for a client concerning a large debt. The client owes Berkin Finance £100,000 and is being pressed to pay the debt. The client agrees to sell his holiday cottage by auction in order to pay the debt. The cottage is valued at £120,000 and the client is hopeful that he will receive at least this price at the auction.

Berkin Finance writes to the client stating that unless the debt is paid in full within seven days, it will commence court proceedings. As the auction is to be held in 10 days' time, Ayesha (acting on the instructions of the client) undertakes to Berkin Finance to pay £100,000 from the proceeds of sale of the cottage.

The cottage is sold at auction for £90,000. Berkin Finance demands the full £100,000 from Ayesha. Ayesha must perform the undertaking given by her and pay the full amount (ie £100,000), irrespective of the fact that the proceeds of sale are insufficient.

Ayesha should have drafted the undertaking to state clearly that her liability would be limited to the money she received from the sale.

The Law Society has agreed standard wording for undertakings which commonly arise in practice, for example an undertaking required from the seller's solicitor in a conveyancing transaction to discharge the mortgage over the property on completion. Even when presented with an undertaking on the 'standard' form, the solicitor must check the wording carefully in the light of the particular transaction to ensure that it is appropriate.

8.5.1 Acts outside the solicitor's control

A solicitor may be called upon to undertake to perform an act which is outside the solicitor's control, such as to forward documents which are not in the solicitor's possession. The simple fact that the solicitor is unable to perform the undertaking without the cooperation of the client or another third party does not discharge the solicitor's obligation to perform, and the undertaking remains enforceable.

Providing an undertaking which is wholly reliant on the action/inaction of a third party should be avoided given the binding nature of such an undertaking. In other appropriate circumstances, a solicitor may seek to give an undertaking that, in respect of the example above, they will use their 'reasonable endeavours' to obtain and provide the documents requested. This will impose a lesser obligation upon the solicitor, just as such a 'reasonable endeavours' obligation in contract imposes a lesser obligation on the contracting party. However, it may not give the party who might seek to rely on it the same comfort as an absolute undertaking, and the recipient may therefore choose not to accept it, which may cause delay to the transaction.

8.5.2 Undertakings 'on behalf of' a client

Whilst an undertaking is almost always made for the benefit of the solicitor's client (in order to smooth the transaction as explained above), it is made in the solicitor's name. However, an undertaking may be drafted as being made 'on behalf of' the solicitor's client. This will not prevent the undertaking from being enforceable as against the solicitor, who will remain personally liable.

In theory, it is possible for a solicitor to give an undertaking 'on behalf' of a client and exclude personal liability. In order to do so, the solicitor would have to expressly disclaim personal liability in the very clearest terms. However, an undertaking that seeks to exclude personal liability on behalf of the solicitor is unlikely to be accepted by the proposed recipient, as their ability to enforce it (and therefore rely on it) will be greatly reduced.

8.5.3 Timescale

Paragraph 1.3 expressly provides that undertakings must be performed 'within an agreed timescale', and therefore it is important that any such timescale is expressed when the undertaking is given. Where no timescale has been agreed, however, Paragraph 1.3 provides that the undertaking must be performed within a 'reasonable amount of time'. What is 'reasonable' will depend upon the facts of each case, and so this element of uncertainty should be a consideration when preparing to give or receive such undertakings.

8.5.4 Costs

Where an undertaking is given in respect of the payment of costs of another party, the term 'costs' will be implied to mean proper costs unless a specific amount is agreed. Therefore, a solicitor is able to request an assessment of the costs by the court if costs are not agreed.

8.6 Client's authority

An undertaking is a personal obligation on the solicitor who gave it, and therefore the solicitor will be held liable for it, even if performance would put the solicitor in breach of his duty to the client. A solicitor must have clear and express authority from the client before giving any undertakings. When such authority has been received, it may be withdrawn by the client at any time until the solicitor has acted upon it, even if it is expressed to be irrevocable.

⭐ *Example*

Meredith, a solicitor, is instructed by a landlord regarding the renewal of a lease of a domestic property. Meredith is told that the landlord is very keen to retain the existing tenant, rather than going to the expense of advertising the property and having it stand empty for possibly weeks whilst a new tenant is found.

Meredith is told that the tenant will attend her office tomorrow (the day the lease is due to expire), to 'tie up a few loose ends' and sign a new tenancy agreement.

The following day the tenant duly arrives at Meredith's office. However, it soon becomes clear that there are problems to be resolved before the tenant will agree to the new tenancy. The tenant explains that the house is in a shabby state, and the only way that the tenant would be willing to agree to a new tenancy is if the landlord agrees to redecorate the entire house and fit new carpets.

Meredith tries to negotiate with the tenant that the landlord will look at the matter after the new lease is signed. However, the tenant states that unless the issues are dealt with today, they will terminate the existing lease and rent some other property. Meredith is unable to contact the landlord and so reluctantly gives an undertaking on behalf of the landlord that the property will be redecorated and the carpets replaced within one month. The tenant happily renews the lease.

Meredith informs her client of the undertaking the next day. The landlord is outraged, and refuses to carry out the work.

The undertaking was given on behalf of a client, but as Meredith did not expressly disclaim personal liability, she will be bound to comply with the undertaking. The tenant can enforce the undertaking by suing Meredith. If the client maintains their stance and refuses to comply, Meredith will personally have to pay for the redecoration and carpets and ensure that this is done within the timescale stated. In addition to being sued by the tenant, Meredith could also be reported to the SRA and the Legal Ombudsman in the form of a complaint about the services provided by her.

Meredith should not have given the undertaking without obtaining her client's authority and consent.

8.7 Change of circumstances

An undertaking will remain binding upon the solicitor if the circumstances change so that it is impossible to fulfil it, either wholly or partially. However, the recipient may agree to its variation or discharge. Where an undertaking is given which is dependent upon the happening of a future event and it becomes apparent that the future event in question will not occur, good practice will be to notify the recipient of this.

8.8 Enforcement

8.8.1 The courts

The court has a supervisory role in respect of a solicitor as an officer of the court. The court's inherent jurisdiction in this regard has its roots in history but is now contained in s 50 of the Solicitors Act 1974. The court can therefore enforce a solicitor's undertaking against an individual solicitor or an unincorporated law practice. Accordingly, where a solicitor's undertaking has been breached, an aggrieved party may seek summary enforcement or compensation for any loss. Firms are obliged to carry indemnity insurance to cover such claims. However, the value of such claims may well fall within the excess of those policies, leading to personal liability for the solicitor concerned.

The fact that an undertaking was given by a solicitor does not make it a 'solicitor's undertaking' capable of enforcement by the court. A 'solicitor's undertaking' for these purposes must have been given by an individual in their capacity as a solicitor (as opposed to in a personal or business capacity). The rationale is that the court's inherent jurisdiction is aimed a disciplining those performing the role of a solicitor. However, in practice most undertakings will satisfy this requirement.

In *Harcus Sinclair v Your Lawyers* [2021] UKSC 32, the Supreme Court confirmed that an undertaking given by an incorporated law practice, ie a limited company or LLP (or an undertaking given by an individual solicitor as agent for such a practice), is not capable of being enforced against that practice by the court under its inherent jurisdiction. This is because an incorporated practice is a separate legal entity. This case has highlighted a sharp divide on the enforcement of undertakings which Parliament may or may not address in due course. Certainly, for the time being, individual solicitors should refer to their firm's policy on accepting undertakings from incorporated practices.

Where an undertaking is not enforceable by the court, the redress for its breach will be a claim under contract, negligence or breach of statutory trust depending on the facts.

A breach of any undertaking is likely to be a breach of professional conduct. However, given the court's jurisdiction over solicitors concerning undertakings, the SRA does not usually investigate a breach of an undertaking given to the court itself, unless the court reported the matter to the SRA.

8.8.2 The SRA and the Solicitors Disciplinary Tribunal

As the SRA makes clear in its guidance on undertakings, breach of an undertaking by individuals and firms (including solicitors and incorporated practices) is a breach of professional conduct. The Legal Ombudsman, the SRA and the Solicitors Disciplinary Tribunal have no power to enforce the performance of an undertaking. Neither can these organisations direct that a solicitor pay compensation to an aggrieved third party. However, they may investigate the matter and impose disciplinary sanctions, as appropriate, against the solicitor, the firm, its members or directors (up to and including, in the case of the Solicitors Disciplinary Tribunal, striking a solicitor off the roll of solicitors).

Summary

- An undertaking is any statement, whether or not it includes the word 'undertake' or 'undertaking', made by or on behalf of a solicitor or their firm to someone who reasonably places reliance upon it, that the giver of the statement or a third party will do something or cause something to be done, or refrain from doing something.

- A solicitor will be personally bound to honour an undertaking, regardless of whether the undertaking was given orally or in writing.

- Any ambiguity in the wording of an undertaking is likely to be construed against the party that gave it.

- A solicitor should obtain the client's express authority before giving an undertaking.

- A solicitor's undertaking may be enforced by the court.

- The SRA/Legal Ombudsman/Solicitors Disciplinary Tribunal do not have the power to enforce an undertaking. However, any breach of an undertaking may be considered a breach of professional conduct, or result in a complaint about services provided by a solicitor which may lead to sanctions against the solicitor concerned.

Sample questions

Question 1

A solicitor works for an unincorporated law firm. The solicitor is acting for the buyer in a protracted residential conveyancing matter. The solicitor receives a telephone call from the seller (who is unrepresented). The seller is becoming increasingly frustrated at the delay and threatens to pull out of the deal. To prevent this, the solicitor says to the seller, 'My firm will pay the deposit of £20,000 to you by 10 am tomorrow.'

Which of the following statements best explains who is liable to pay the £20,000?

A   Neither the solicitor nor the firm are liable because the solicitor did not use the word 'undertake' when speaking to the seller.

B   The firm is liable, but not the solicitor, because this was an undertaking expressly made on the firm's behalf.

C   The firm is liable, but not the solicitor, because the solicitor was acting in the best interests of the client.

D   The solicitor is liable, but not the firm, because an undertaking is only binding on the person who gave it.

E   Both the solicitor and the firm are liable, because the statement made by the solicitor amounts to an undertaking binding on both the individual and the firm.

Answer

Option E is correct. The statement is an undertaking even though the word 'undertaking' is not used (option A is therefore wrong). The SRA Glossary definition makes it clear that it is not necessary to include the word 'undertake' for an oral or written statement, on which reliance is placed, to constitute an enforceable promise. The undertaking is binding both on the individual and the firm. The fact that the solicitor was motivated by trying to save the deal does not exclude the solicitor from liability.

Question 2

A solicitor is in practice as a sole practitioner. The solicitor is acting for a client in a litigation matter. At the hearing, the client loses the case and is ordered to pay £5,000 towards the opponent's costs. Outside court the solicitor says to their opponent, 'Don't worry. I'll make sure that the £5,000 will be paid within the next 14 days.' Fourteen days have now elapsed and the client has still not provided the solicitor with any funds to pay the costs.

Who can force the solicitor to comply with the promise?

A   The Solicitors' Regulatory Authority.

B   The Solicitors' Disciplinary Tribunal.

C   The Legal Ombudsman.

D   The court.

E   No one.

Answer

Option D is correct. The solicitor's statement would amount to a solicitor's undertaking and the solicitor has not complied with its terms. Whilst a failure to perform an undertaking may result in disciplinary proceedings being taken against the solicitor, only the court has the power to enforce a solicitor's undertaking.

Question 3

A solicitor is acting for the seller in a residential conveyancing transaction. At 5 pm, the solicitor receives a telephone call from the buyer's solicitors to say that in breach of their agreement, the seller has failed to finish some repairs to the property. Completion is due to take place the following morning and the buyer is threatening to pull out of the transaction unless the repairs are completed. To ensure that the transaction proceeds, the solicitor confirms to the buyer's solicitor that the seller will carry out the repairs before completion.

The solicitor immediately telephones the seller. The seller's voicemail message says the seller has been unexpectedly called away on business and cannot be contacted until tomorrow afternoon.

Which of the following best explains the solicitor's professional conduct position?

A   The solicitor has given an undertaking which is binding upon the solicitor personally.

B   The solicitor has acted dishonestly in making a promise which could not be met.

C   There are no professional conduct issues because the promise was that it would be the client, rather than the solicitor, who would carry out the repairs.

D   There are no professional conduct issues because the telephone conversation was not confirmed in writing.

E   There are no professional conduct issues because the promise was too ambiguous to be construed as an undertaking.

Answer

Option A is correct.

Option E is wrong. There is no ambiguity in the solicitor's statement (and in any event any ambiguity is likely to be resolved in favour of the recipient). It would be construed as an undertaking.

Option D is wrong. The definition of an undertaking makes it clear that it does not matter that the undertaking was given orally.

Option C is wrong. An undertaking 'on behalf' of a client is binding on the solicitor personally.

The solicitor may have been foolish in giving the undertaking without speaking to the client first, but their behaviour would not be considered dishonest. Option B is therefore wrong.

9 Duties to the Court and Third Parties

SQE1 syllabus

This chapter will help you to achieve the SQE1 Assessment Specification in relation to Functioning Legal Knowledge concerned with Ethics and Professional Conduct on:

- the purpose, scope and content of the SRA Principles,
- the purpose, scope and content of the SRA Code of Conduct for Solicitors, RELs and RFLs.

Ethics and Professional Conduct is a pervasive topic in SQE1 and may be examined across all subject areas.

Note that for SQE1, candidates are not usually required to recall specific case names or cite statutory or regulatory authorities. Cases are provided for illustrative purposes only.

Learning outcomes

By the end of this chapter you will be able to demonstrate your ability to act honestly and with integrity, and in accordance with the SRA Standards and Regulations in relation to:

- dispute resolution and proceedings before courts, tribunals and inquiries;
- maintaining trust and acting fairly; and
- the core requirements of the SRA Principles.

9.1   Introduction

A solicitor's focus will inevitably be on the client: achieving the client's objectives, advancing the client's case and acting in the client's best interests. However, a solicitor must also keep in mind that their duty to the client is not the be-all and end-all. A solicitor also owes duties to the courts, third parties and to the public interest. These wider duties may dictate how a solicitor must act in a given situation.

This chapter looks at:

- duty to the court
- refusal of instructions to act
- instructing counsel
- duties to third parties.

9.2   Duty to the court

A solicitor is an officer of the court. Solicitors have a key part to play in the courts' function within the legal system. As an officer of the court, a solicitor owes a duty to the court.

There are a number of duties and requirements under the SRA Principles and Code for Solicitors that can be said to come under the umbrella of a solicitor's duty to the court.

A solicitor has a duty to act in a way that upholds the constitutional principle of the rule of law and the proper administration of justice (Principle 1). A solicitor also has a duty to act in the best interests of each client (Principle 7). The potential for conflict between these duties can present itself particularly in the context of conducting litigation.

As Lord Hoffman said in *Arthur JS Hall v Simons* [2002] 1 AC 615:

> Lawyers conducting litigation owe a divided loyalty. They have a duty to their clients, but they may not win by whatever means. They also owe a duty to the court and the administration of justice.

The introduction to the SRA Principles makes it clear that, should the Principles come into conflict, those which safeguard the wider public interest take precedence over an individual client's interests. Principle 1 is therefore the overriding duty. The introduction goes on to provide that a solicitor should, where relevant, inform the client of the circumstances in which the solicitor's duty to the court and other professional obligations outweigh his duty to the client.

9.2.1   The duty not to mislead the court

A basic and self-explanatory duty is found in Paragraph 1.4:

> You must not mislead or attempt to mislead the court (or others), either by your own acts or omissions or allowing or being complicit in the acts or omissions of others (including your client).

This duty is part and parcel of the fundamental requirements for a solicitor to act with honesty (Principle 4) and integrity (Principle 5) and uphold public trust in the profession (Principle 2).

Misleading the court can take a wide variety of forms, such as helping a client to create a false alibi or making false statements to the court.

⭐ *Example*

Kim, a solicitor, is representing her client, Carl, in an employment tribunal. Carl was sacked by his employer for allegedly stealing a laptop. Carl is making a claim for unfair dismissal. During cross-examination Carl denies that he ever had the laptop in his possession. Later that day he confides in Kim that he took the laptop and sold it to a friend to fund a holiday.

What should Kim do?

*Kim must not mislead or attempt to mislead the court, or be complicit in another person doing so (including her client). The tribunal is a court for these purposes. Following the conversation, Kim is aware that Carl has committed perjury within the proceedings, and so Kim should refuse to continue to act for Carl unless he agrees to disclose the truth to the tribunal. Kim cannot inform the tribunal of the truth (or her reasons for withdrawal) without the consent of the client as to do so would be a breach of confidentiality (Paragraph 6.3, see **Chapter 6**).*

Paragraph 1.4 is a frequent consideration for solicitors acting for the defence in criminal cases. For example, a solicitor may be faced with a client who admits their guilt to the solicitor during the course of the legal proceedings, but nevertheless insists on pleading not guilty and on giving evidence in the witness box, denying guilt. The duty under Paragraph 1.4 would require the solicitor to decline to act in such circumstances.

Misleading the court is a serious matter. It demonstrates a real want of ethical behaviour. It is therefore likely to result in severe sanctions being imposed on a solicitor. According to Lord Thomas of Cwmgiedd, CJ in *Brett v SRA* [2014] EWHC 2974 (Admin):

> misleading the court is regarded by the court and must be regarded by any disciplinary tribunal as one of the most serious offences that an advocate or litigator can commit. It is not simply a breach of a rule of a game, but a fundamental affront to a rule designed to safeguard the fairness and justice of proceedings. Such conduct will normally attract an exemplary and deterrent sentence.

9.2.2 The conduct of litigation

Being involved in litigation, whether civil or criminal, is a serious matter for any client. Misconduct by a solicitor in this context can therefore have a severe impact on the lives of the individuals involved. However, litigation is such a public and visible aspect of the work of solicitors that any misconduct will almost invariably also undermine trust in the profession and the legal system as a whole.

Paragraphs 2.1 to 2.7 set out some specific obligations in the context of dispute resolution and proceedings before courts, tribunals and inquiries. The SRA Glossary defines 'court' as any court, tribunal or inquiry of England and Wales, or a British court martial, or any court of another jurisdiction. Breaches of these specific provisions may also amount to misleading the court and consequently a breach of Paragraph 1.4.

A solicitor must not misuse or tamper with evidence or attempt to do so (Paragraph 2.1) and must only make assertions or put forward statements, representations or submissions to the court or others which are properly arguable (Paragraph 2.4). Examples of breaches of these duties are wide-ranging and include:

(a) calling a witness whose evidence the solicitor knows is untrue;

(b) continuing to act for a client if the solicitor becomes aware that the client has committed perjury or deliberately misled (or attempted to mislead) the court;

(c) constructing facts to support a client's case or drafting documents relating to proceedings containing statements or contentions which the solicitor does not consider to be properly arguable before a court.

A solicitor must not place themselves in contempt of court and must comply with court orders which place obligations on the solicitor (Paragraph 2.5) and must not waste the court's time (Paragraph 2.6).

An increase in the number of reports to the SRA about misconduct in the conduct litigation resulted in the SRA producing a report in 2018 entitled 'Balancing duties in litigation'. The report outlines various instances of misconduct. In some cases, the solicitor had improperly placed the interests of the client above the solicitor's other duties; in others the solicitor had failed to act in the client's best interests. Subsequently, the SRA published its Guidance on conduct in disputes. Examples include:

(a) Making allegations without merit. This occurs when a solicitor brings a claim with insufficient investigation of the merits or the underlying legal background. There is little or no legal merit, or the solicitor may threaten/initiate litigation in such a case in the hope that the opponent will pay a settlement rather than incur the costs of defending the case.

(b) Pursuing litigation for improper purposes. This occurs when a solicitor uses the court process for purposes not directly connected to resolving a dispute, for example to run up high costs for the client's commercial rival or silencing criticism.

(c) Conducting excessive or aggressive litigation.

A particular concern in relation to litigation misconduct that has emerged in recent years are so-called Strategic Lawsuits against Public Participation (SLAPPs). In essence a SLAPP involves the bringing or threatening of proceedings as a means of intimidation or harassment. The aim is to stop the 'target' publishing information relating to a matter of public interest, such as whistle-blowing or the results of investigative journalism. SLAPPs can take a variety of forms, but typically involve bringing/threatening proceedings for defamation or misuse of information (for more detail, see the SRA Warning Notice, 30 May 2024).

9.2.3 Witnesses

A solicitor will frequently seek to gather evidence by interviewing witnesses. Should a solicitor wish, or require, in the best interests of the client, to take statements from a witness or potential witness, the solicitor may do so at any point in the proceedings. This remains the case whether or not that individual has already been interviewed by another party or has been called as a witness by another party.

A solicitor must not seek to influence the substance of evidence, including generating false evidence or persuading witnesses to change their evidence (Paragraph 2.2). In the report, 'Balancing duties in litigation', the SRA cited examples of such behaviour being reported, including where solicitors have knowingly helped criminal clients to create a false alibi and, where they have known that their client has obtained information to help their case by illegal means, helped them provide a false explanation as to where it came from.

A solicitor must not provide or offer to provide any benefit to witnesses dependent upon the nature of their evidence or the outcome of the case (Paragraph 2.3).

To avoid any suggestion of impropriety, it may be prudent to interview a witness in the presence of their legal representative.

9.2.4 Duty to disclose law and facts

A solicitor who appears before the court for the defence in a criminal case, or for either party in a civil case, has no duty to inform the court of any evidence or witnesses which would prejudice the solicitor's own client.

However, there is a duty on the part of a solicitor to draw the court's attention to relevant cases and statutory provisions or procedural irregularities of which the solicitor is aware and which are likely to have a material effect on the outcome of the proceedings (Paragraph 2.7). Clearly, drawing such matters to the attention of the court may work against the client's case. However, this is a situation in which the duty to uphold the rule of law and the proper administration of justice is likely to take precedence.

Different considerations apply to a solicitor who appears before the court for the prosecution in a criminal case. The requirement placed on the prosecution to present evidence in a dispassionate manner means that in addition to complying with the duty under Paragraph 2.7, the solicitor must, for example, put all relevant facts before the court and notify the defence of evidence which may assist the defendant.

9.3 Refusing instructions to act

A solicitor is never obliged to act in a case. A solicitor is generally free to decide whether or not to accept instructions in any matter, provided that the solicitor does not discriminate unlawfully (see **4.3**).

If it is clear to a solicitor appearing as an advocate, or acting in litigation, that the solicitor or anyone else in the firm will be called as a witness in the matter, the solicitor should decline to appear/act unless satisfied that this will not prejudice the solicitor's independence as an advocate or a litigator (Principle 3), the interests of the client (Principle 7) or the interests of justice (Principle 1).

9.4 Instructing counsel

A solicitor conducting a litigation matter will often wish to instruct counsel to represent the client as advocate in court hearings. However, instructing counsel should not be done automatically or as a matter of routine. A solicitor is obliged to act in the best interests of the client (Principle 7) and ensure that the service provided is competent and delivered in a timely manner (Paragraph 3.2). Accordingly, where the client requires advocacy services, the solicitor must consider, based on the complexity of the case and the solicitor's own experience, whether it would be in the best interests of that client to instruct counsel (or another solicitor within the firm) to act as the advocate in the proceedings.

9.4.1 Choice of advocate

A solicitor must exercise care in choosing the appropriate barrister for the case, taking into consideration the experience and seniority of counsel available.

In selecting a particular barrister, a solicitor must not discriminate by allowing their personal views to affect their professional relationships and the way in which the solicitor provides services (Paragraph 1.1) and must act in a way that encourages equality, diversity and inclusion (Principle 6). Consequently, a solicitor must not discriminate when instructing a barrister on the grounds of, for example, age, race, sex or disability. Indeed, it is unlawful for a solicitor to do so under s 47 Equality Act 2010.

A solicitor may consult with the client when choosing a barrister, however the solicitor must consider the motivation behind any input from the client. The client's request may appear to be based on discriminatory grounds. For example, a male client defending himself in an employment tribunal against an allegation of sex discrimination may request to be represented by a female advocate. In such circumstances, the solicitor should discuss the issue with the client and, if necessary, ask the client to change their instructions. Where the client refuses, it will usually be appropriate for the solicitor to cease to act.

9.4.2 Duty to counsel

If it is in the client's best interests to instruct counsel, it remains the solicitor's duty to ensure that adequate instructions are provided to the chosen barrister. As an extension of the solicitor's duty to the client, the solicitor should ensure that these instructions, including any relevant supporting statements, information or documents, are provided in good time to allow adequate preparation of the case.

In order to provide such information, it may be necessary, if practicable, to arrange a conference with counsel, either with or without the client, to enable the barrister to discuss directly the nature of the case, obtain instructions or further information and provide advice in a direct manner. It is a matter for the solicitor to ascertain whether such a conference would be appropriate, and in the client's best interests, and if so, to arrange it.

9.4.3 Duty to the client

Notwithstanding the appointment of counsel and the duties the chosen barrister may owe to a solicitor's client, all the solicitor's duties to the client remain in full force and effect. Instructing counsel does not relieve the solicitor of those duties, particularly the duty to act in the best interests of the client.

When instructing counsel, the solicitor must be satisfied with the quality of the advice given and ensure that there are no obvious errors or inconsistencies. If such errors are apparent, clarification should be requested or a second opinion obtained. According to Mr Justice Simon in *Regent Leisuretime v Skerrett* [2005] EWHC 2255 (QB):

> in general, a solicitor is entitled to rely upon the advice of counsel properly instructed however, the solicitor must not rely on such advice without exercising his own independent judgement. If he thinks the advice is obviously wrong, it is his duty to reject it.

9.4.4 Counsel's fees

A solicitor is responsible for appointing counsel and (subject to limited exceptions) is therefore responsible personally for the payment of counsel's fees. This applies regardless of whether the solicitor's client has provided the requisite monies. Many solicitors therefore request that their clients provide money on account to cover prospective barristers' fees.

✪ Example

Liam, a solicitor, instructs counsel on behalf of a client, Ryan, to provide advice on a particular legal issue. Counsel's fee is £1,000 plus VAT. Before Liam can issue a bill, Ryan is declared bankrupt.

Who is responsible for the counsel's fee?

Liam. This is why many solicitors request that their clients provide them with money on account before instructing counsel.

9.5 Duties to third parties

A solicitor's duties are primarily owed to the client and the court. However, in certain circumstances a solicitor also has a duty to third parties or the rules of professional conduct require a solicitor to behave in a certain way towards third parties.

9.5.1 Not taking an unfair advantage

Under Paragraph 1.2 a solicitor must not abuse their position by taking unfair advantage of not only the client, but also others. Although of general application, this Principle may be of particular relevance in the context of dispute resolution and conducting proceedings before the court.

Third parties may well have a lack of legal knowledge or proper understanding of legal procedures, and a solicitor must not seek to take unfair advantage of this in pursuing a case for a client. Particular care must be taken in situations where the opponent is unrepresented or is vulnerable, for example due to age or mental capacity. The SRA in its report 'Balancing duties in litigation' conceded that there can be a 'fine line between proper defence of the client's interest and taking unfair advantage of others, usually highlighted by any form of deceit or misinformation'. Specific examples of conduct reported to the SRA in this context include overbearing threats of claims or poor outcomes, legalistic letters to minors or others who might be vulnerable and threats of litigation where no legal claims arises. Additionally, the SRA has issued a warning notice on the use of non-disclosure agreements (NDAs) following concerns about their improper use, for example, in relation to allegations of harassment.

The SRA views the protection of the vulnerable as an important part of its role. The Enforcement Strategy makes clear that the SRA will consider an allegation to be 'particularly serious' where the vulnerability of the client or third party is relevant to the solicitor's behaviour.

9.5.2 Public office and personal interests

Solicitors may sometimes be appointed to a public office, such as being a member of a planning committee or a district judge. The public office may provide the solicitor with confidential information or inside knowledge of, for example, policy, which may affect the solicitor's advice to a client or the solicitor's approach to the matter.

The 'inside information' might also be available to the solicitor if another individual at the solicitor's practice (whether partner, member or employee) held such an office, or indeed if it was held by a member of the solicitor's family.

If a solicitor takes unfair advantage of a public office held by the solicitor, a member of their family or their firm, it is unlikely that the solicitor will be acting in a way that upholds public trust and confidence in the solicitors' profession or with integrity. This would place the solicitor in breach of Principles 2 and 5.

9.5.3 Giving references

A solicitor may be asked to provide references for employees in respect of future employment. Under the general law of negligence, a solicitor will owe a duty of care to the subject of any reference given by that solicitor. Although not a case involving solicitors, in *Spring v Guardian Assurance plc* [1994] 3 All ER 129, the House of Lords held that an employer who provided a reference in respect of an employee to a prospective future employer owed a duty of care to the employee in respect of the preparation of the reference and was liable in damages for economic loss suffered as a result of the negligent preparation of the reference.

Accordingly, great care must be taken when giving any such reference to avoid incurring liability. Many firms have in place policies with regard to the giving of references, covering who may give them and the nature of the content.

Giving a false reference would almost certainly breach the Code of Conduct for Solicitors, for example for damaging the public trust and confidence in the solicitors' profession (Principle 2).

9.5.4 Offensive communications

The very nature of a solicitor's practice requires communication with a whole variety of third parties. Surveyors, medical experts, the police, social services and other solicitors are just a few examples. A solicitor is under a duty to act with integrity (Principle 5) and in a way that upholds public trust and confidence in the solicitors' profession (Principle 2). Accordingly, a solicitor must not communicate with any third party in a manner that could be considered to be offensive (see **2.4**).

Clearly, communications that are racist or sexist will fall foul of the SRA Principles. However, a communication does not have to be discriminatory in order to be offensive. In its Warning Notice on offensive communications, the SRA says that a solicitor must, for example, guard against robust communications with an opponent crossing the line and becoming offensive.

This could occur, for example, if a solicitor were to pass on or be seen to endorse derogatory remarks made by the client. Similarly, a solicitor should not allow their independence to be compromised by employing abusive or inflammatory language at the client's behest.

9.5.5 Beneficiaries

Where a solicitor is instructed to administer an estate, the solicitor's client will be the personal representative of the deceased's estate. However, in certain circumstances a solicitor will also owe a duty of care to the beneficiaries of that estate.

Ross v Caunters [1980] 1 Ch 297

A solicitor failed to warn a testator that the will should not be witnessed by a beneficiary. Accordingly, the beneficiary who witnessed the will was unable to claim her share of the estate. The solicitor was held liable in negligence to the beneficiary.

White v Jones [1995] 1 All ER 891

A solicitor was instructed to draw up a will. The client died approximately a month later, before the will had been drafted. The solicitor was successfully sued in negligence by the beneficiaries who missed out on their share of the estate as a result of the solicitor's failure to draft the will.

9.5.6 Contacting a represented third party

Where a client instructs a solicitor, it is often because the client lacks legal knowledge and skills and therefore seeks the assistance of a legal expert. Care must be taken, therefore, in the context of a solicitor communicating with another party when the solicitor is aware that the other party has retained a lawyer in a matter. There is nothing specific in the Code of Conduct for Solicitors dealing with this situation; it will be prudent to avoid such communication except:

(a) to request the name and address of the other party's lawyer; or

(b) where the other party's lawyer consents to the solicitor communicating with the client; or

(c) where there are exceptional circumstances.

9.5.7 Agents' costs

As with counsel's fees, a solicitor is personally responsible for meeting the fees of agents or others appointed by the solicitor on behalf of the client. This extends only to costs properly incurred. Again, this applies whether or not the solicitor has been put in funds, and therefore the solicitor may ask for monies on account prior to incurring such expenditure. Alternatively, the solicitor and agent may agree that the agent's fee will become payable on receipt by the solicitor of the client's payment.

Summary

- A solicitor must not mislead or attempt to mislead the court or allow or be complicit in others doing so (including the client). A solicitor must also not place themselves in contempt of court and must comply with any order of the court.

- A solicitor must not offer to provide any benefits to witnesses dependent upon their evidence or the outcome of the case.

- A solicitor must not misuse or tamper with evidence or influence the substance of evidence, including generating false evidence or persuading witnesses to change their evidence.

- There is a duty on a solicitor to draw the court's attention to relevant cases and statutory provisions or procedural irregularities of which the solicitor is aware and which are likely to have a material effect on the outcome of the proceedings.

- A solicitor still owes the client a duty to act in the client's best interests even when the solicitor has instructed counsel to act for that client.

- A solicitor must not take unfair advantage of clients or others.

- A solicitor will be breaching the Principles if the solicitor takes unfair advantage of a public office.

- In certain circumstances a solicitor owes a duty of care to third parties, such as beneficiaries.

Sample questions

Question 1

A solicitor is acting for a client on a plea of guilty to a charge of assault on a member of staff in a public house. At the sentencing hearing the court asks the solicitor to confirm that the client's list of previous convictions is accurate. The client instructs the solicitor to confirm that the list is accurate despite the fact a conviction for assaulting a bartender last year has been omitted. The solicitor advises the client that this omission should be corrected, but the client does not want to do this.

Which of the following best explains what the solicitor should do?

A   Tell the client that the solicitor must cease to act because the solicitor cannot knowingly mislead the court.

B   Do as the client instructs because the solicitor's duty to act in the best interests of the client overrides the solicitor's duty not to mislead the court.

C   Continue to act but tell the court that the list is inaccurate because keeping quiet would be a breach of the solicitor's duty to act in a way which upholds the proper administration of justice.

D   Correct the list and then cease to act because this accords with the solicitor's duty to uphold the proper administration of justice.

E   Continue to act but refuse to confirm or deny the accuracy of the list because the solicitor will not mislead the court by remaining silent.

Answer

Option A is correct. The solicitor cannot continue to act knowing that the list is inaccurate as this would be misleading the court (Paragraph 1.4). However, the solicitor cannot disclose confidential information without the client's consent (Paragraph 6.3). Hence, the solicitor would have to cease to act, without correcting the list.

Question 2

A solicitor is acting for the defendant in a criminal case. The solicitor interviews a potential witness. During the course of the interview, it transpires that the witness' evidence works against the defendant's case.

Which of the following best describes how the solicitor's duties apply in this situation?

A   The solicitor's duty to act in the client's best interests requires that the solicitor try to persuade the witness to change their evidence.

B   The solicitor is not obliged to call the witness, but the solicitor must be careful to adhere to the solicitor's duty not to mislead the court.

C   The solicitor's duty to uphold the administration of justice requires the solicitor to call the witness regardless of the evidence the witness will give.

D   The solicitor is under a duty to draw the court's attention to the witness' evidence because it is likely to have a material effect on the outcome of the case.

E   The solicitor's duty to act with integrity requires the solicitor to tell the prosecution about the witness' evidence.

Answer

Option B is correct There is no obligation to call the witness (option C therefore is wrong), but Paragraph 1.4 requires that a solicitor does not mislead the court. Option D is wrong as there is no duty to inform the court of evidence which prejudices the solicitor's client (cf. cases, statutes and procedural irregularities in Paragraph 2.7). Option A is wrong as trying to persuade the witness to change their evidence would breach Paragraph 2.2. There is no duty to inform the prosecution of a potential witness' evidence and therefore option E is also wrong.

Question 3

A solicitor is acting for the claimant in a litigation matter. The defendant is unrepresented. On the journey to court for the final hearing the solicitor is reading a legal journal and discovers that the solicitor has overlooked a case which completely destroys the client's case.

What should the solicitor do on arrival at court?

A   Cease to act.

B   Provide the defendant with the name of the case and its citation.

C   Draw the court's attention to the case.

D   Ask for the client's consent to the solicitor drawing the case to the court's attention.

E   Tell the client that the case cannot proceed because of a procedural irregularity.

Answer

Option C is correct. Under Paragraph 2.7 a solicitor is under a duty to draw the court's attention to cases which are likely to have a material effect on the case. Compliance with the duty is not dependent on the client's consent (option D is wrong). Immediately ceasing to act would not assist the client, and would not comply with Paragraph 2.7; option A is therefore not the best answer. Option B is not the best answer, as providing details of the case would not assist an unrepresented party and may be considered to be taking unfair advantage of a third party. Option E is wrong – the solicitor must draw the court's attention to the case. What that means for the ongoing conduct of the final hearing will ultimately be a matter for the court (unless the claimant decides to discontinue its claim).

10 Duties to the SRA and Compliance

SQE1 syllabus

This chapter will help you to achieve the SQE1 Assessment Specification in relation to Functioning Legal Knowledge concerned with Ethics and Professional Conduct on:

- the purpose, scope and content of the SRA Code of Conduct for Solicitors, RELs and RFLs,

- the purpose, scope and content of the SRA Code of Conduct for Firms in relation to managers in authorised firms and compliance officers.

Ethics and Professional Conduct is a pervasive topic in SQE1 and may be examined across all subject areas.

Note that for SQE1, candidates are not usually required to recall specific case names or cite statutory or regulatory authorities.

Learning outcomes

By the end of this chapter you will be able to demonstrate your ability to act honestly and with integrity, and in accordance with the SRA Standards and Regulations in relation to:

- cooperation and accountability;

- managers in SRA-authorised firms; and

- compliance officers.

10.1 Introduction

It is in every solicitor's interests for the profession to employ ethical behaviour. If one individual falls short of the required standard this reflects on the profession as a whole. To that end, all solicitors are under a duty to work with the SRA in ensuring that not only their own conduct, but also the conduct of those with whom they work or come into contact, meets high standards.

This chapter looks at:

- keeping up to date
- cooperation
- investigating claims for redress
- notification
- reporting
- reporting to compliance officers
- miscellaneous business requirements
- managers
- compliance officers.

10.2 Keeping up to date

A basic requirement is set out in Paragraph 7.1 which provides that a solicitor must keep up to date with and follow the law and regulation governing the way the solicitor works. Despite this requirement, in its Review of Professional Obligations (13 December 2024), the SRA identified a lack of regulatory knowledge amongst solicitors. It expressed concern that individuals were too reliant on others within the firm (such as compliance officers – see **10.10**) to disseminate regulatory information. The SRA issued a reminder that each solicitor is individually accountable for compliance with regulatory requirements.

Every solicitor must keep abreast of the relevant provisions of legislation affecting practice, such as the Solicitors Act 1974 and the Legal Services Act 2007. Solicitors must also have and maintain knowledge and understanding of the SRA Standards and Regulations (in particular the Principles, Codes of Conduct and the Accounts Rules) and the Guidance issued by the SRA designed to help solicitors understand the obligations placed upon them.

10.3 Cooperation

During the course of their practice, a solicitor will inevitably have dealings with the SRA from time to time. This may be for a variety of reasons such as when applying for an assessment of character and suitability or applying for admission to the Roll. At the most extreme, a solicitor may be contacted by the SRA because the SRA is carrying out an investigation into the conduct of the solicitor or their firm.

A solicitor must cooperate with the SRA as well as other regulators, ombudsmen, and those bodies with a role overseeing and supervising the delivery of, or investigating concerns in relation to, legal services (Paragraph 7.3). A solicitor must also respond promptly to the SRA and provide full and accurate explanations, information and documents in response to any request or requirement and ensure that relevant information is available for inspection by the SRA (Paragraph 7.4). Such information may be required where the SRA is investigating whether the solicitor is complying with the requirements of professional conduct. Any remedial action requested by the SRA must be acted upon promptly (Paragraph 7.10).

10.4 Investigating claims for redress

A solicitor must be 'honest and open' with clients if things go wrong and, if a client suffers loss or harm as a result, put matters right (if possible) and explain fully and promptly to the client what has happened and the likely impact. If required to do so by the SRA, the solicitor must investigate whether anyone may have a claim against them, provide the SRA with a report on the outcome of the investigation and notify relevant persons that they may have such a claim accordingly (Paragraph 7.11).

10.5 Notification

Paragraph 7.6 requires a solicitor to notify the SRA automatically should a particular event occur. The notification requirement arises if:

(a) the solicitor is subject to a criminal charge, conviction or caution;

(b) the solicitor is made bankrupt, enters an individual voluntary arrangement with their creditors or is subject to a debt relief order;

(c) the solicitor becomes aware of material change in information about them or their practice previously provided to the SRA;

(d) the solicitor becomes aware that information previously provided to the SRA about them or their practice is false, misleading, incomplete or inaccurate.

10.6 Reporting

The SRA cannot carry out its regulatory role, particularly in terms of enforcing professional standards, unless failures in meeting those standards are brought to its attention. In many cases the SRA will be alerted to potential misconduct by clients making a complaint. However, there is also an obligation placed on solicitors to report such matters themselves. The SRA considers that by reporting behaviour which puts the client, the public or the public interest at risk, a solicitor is fulfilling the duty to act with integrity (Principle 5).

A solicitor is obliged to ensure that a prompt report is made to the SRA of any serious breach of its regulatory arrangements by any person regulated by it (including the solicitor themselves) of which the solicitor is aware (Paragraph 7.7). The obligation to report may also be satisfied by reporting to the firm's compliance officers, where appropriate (Paragraph 7.12) (see **10.7**).

Unlike the notification requirements which arise automatically on the happening of a given event, the reporting obligation will require the solicitor to exercise their own judgment in deciding whether the particular facts require a report to be made.

A report is required in respect of 'a serious breach'. It is clear, therefore, that the SRA will not be concerned with trivial matters or technical breaches. The SRA Enforcement Strategy gives guidance on what types of behaviour the SRA considers to be 'serious'. Factors which the SRA takes into account in assessing seriousness include:

(a) The nature of the allegation

Allegations involving sexual or violent misconduct, dishonesty, criminal behaviour, abuse of trust, taking unfair advantage of clients or others and the misuse of client money are serious in themselves.

(b) Intent/motivation

Conduct which is deliberate, premeditated, dishonest, repeated or displays a reckless disregard of professional obligations is considered to be more serious.

(c) Harm and impact

The greater the harm caused and the more foreseeable the impact, the more likely the behaviour is to be considered serious.

(d) Vulnerability

The SRA understandably takes a particularly poor view of conduct where the 'victim' is vulnerable.

In addition to the obligation to report in Paragraph 7.7, a solicitor must inform the SRA promptly of any matters which the solicitor reasonably believes should be brought to the SRA's attention in order that the SRA can investigate whether a serious breach of its regulatory arrangements has occurred or otherwise exercise its regulatory powers (Paragraph 7.8).

It may be that in making a report or providing information to the SRA a solicitor will be required to disclose matters which would otherwise be regarded as confidential. Here, a solicitor will be required to carry out a careful balancing exercise between the duty of confidentiality (see **Chapter 6**) on the one hand and the public interest on the other. The SRA's view is that the public interest in reporting misconduct, to enable the SRA to discharge its regulatory function, creates a situation in which the disclosure of confidential information is likely to be justified.

In order to ensure that information is passed to the SRA, Paragraph 7.5 provides that a solicitor must not attempt to prevent anyone from providing information to the SRA or any other body exercising regulatory, supervisory, investigatory or prosecutory functions in the public interest.

10.7 Reporting to compliance officers

Under Paragraph 7.12, any obligation placed on a solicitor to notify or provide information to the SRA will be satisfied if the solicitor provides the information to their firm's compliance officers. This will usually be the best option for an individual solicitor. The compliance officers have the ability to investigate the circumstances fully before concluding that the SRA must become involved. However, Paragraph 7.12 does not absolve the solicitor of all responsibility. The solicitor should still make a report themselves if they are convinced that a report is required and are not satisfied that the compliance officers will do so.

10.8 Miscellaneous business requirements

Paragraph 5.5 requires a solicitor who holds a practising certificate to complete and deliver an annual return to the SRA.

Paragraph 5.6 requires a solicitor carrying on reserved legal activities in a non-commercial body to ensure that the body takes out and maintains adequate and appropriate indemnity insurance in compliance with the SRA Indemnity Insurance Rules (see **Legal Services**).

10.9 Managers

Under Paragraph 8.1 of the SRA Code of Conduct for Firms, the responsibility for ensuring the firm's compliance with the Code lies with its managers. Who is a manager will depend on the structure of the business: a sole practitioner, a partner in a partnership, a member of LLP, a director of a company or a member of a governing body.

Managers therefore have the ultimate responsibility for how the firm is run and the legal services delivered. Managers must ensure that the firm complies with all legislative and regulatory requirements. However, a finding of misconduct against a firm by the SRA is not a finding against an individual manager. A manager will generally only be considered to be responsible for their personal actions or if they should have known about or intervened to prevent the wrongdoing.

10.10 Compliance officers

Every firm must have a compliance officer for legal practice (COLP) and a compliance officer for finance and administration (COFA). For sole practitioners and small firms these roles may be fulfilled by the same person. Otherwise, the compliance officers will be senior individuals within the firm approved by the SRA for carrying out this role.

10.10.1 COLP

In essence, a COLP has a wide-ranging responsibility to ensure that systems and controls are in place to enable the firm and those within it to comply with their obligations under the SRA Standards and Regulations, the firm's authorisation from the SRA and relevant statutory provisions (eg the Legal Services Act 2007 and the Solicitors Act 1974).

Under Paragraph 9.1 of the Code of Conduct for Firms a COLP must take all reasonable steps to:

(a) ensure compliance with the terms and conditions of the firm's authorisation;

(b) ensure compliance by the firm and its managers, employees or interest holders with the SRA's regulatory arrangements which apply to them;

(c) ensure that the firm's managers and interest holders and those they employ or contract with do not cause or substantially contribute to a breach of the SRA's regulatory arrangements;

(d) ensure that a prompt report is made to the SRA of any facts or matters that the COLP reasonably believes are capable of amounting to a serious breach of the terms and conditions of the firm's authorisation, or the SRA's regulatory arrangements which apply to the firm, managers or employees;

(e) ensure that the SRA is informed promptly of any facts or matters that the COLP reasonably believes should be brought to its attention in order that it may investigate whether a serious breach of its regulatory arrangements has occurred or otherwise exercise its regulatory powers.

The requirements in (d) and (e) replicate Paragraphs 7.7 and 7.8 of the SRA Code of Conduct for Solicitors, RELs and RFLs. So, where an individual solicitor reports their concerns about misconduct to the COLP, it is for the COLP to pass these on, if appropriate, to the SRA.

Whilst the responsibilities placed on the COLP are wide, the SRA have repeatedly said that the COLP will not be used as a scapegoat for wrongdoing by the firm. The responsibility for compliance ultimately rests with the managers of the practice under Paragraph 8.1 of the SRA Code of Conduct for Firms. However, the COLP may be liable if they fail to meet their own responsibilities.

10.10.2 COFA

Essentially, the firm's COFA fulfils the same role as the COLP but in relation to compliance with the SRA Accounts Rules.

Under Paragraph 9.2 of the SRA Code of Conduct for Firms, a COFA must take all reasonable steps to:

(a) ensure that the firm and its managers and employees comply with any obligations imposed upon them under the SRA Accounts Rules;

(b) ensure that a prompt report is made to the SRA of any facts or matters that the COFA reasonably believes are capable of amounting to a serious breach of the SRA Accounts Rules which apply to them;

(c) ensure that the SRA is informed promptly of any facts or matters that the COFA reasonably believes should be brought to its attention in order that it may investigate whether a serious breach of its regulatory arrangements has occurred or otherwise exercise its regulatory powers.

Again, the responsibility for compliance ultimately rests with the managers of the practice under Paragraph 8.1 of the SRA Code of Conduct for Firms. However, the COFA may be liable if they fail to meet their own responsibilities.

Summary

- A solicitor must keep up to date with law and regulation affecting the way they work.
- A solicitor must cooperate with the SRA, notify the SRA of certain information and report serious breaches of regulatory requirements to the SRA.
- A solicitor's obligation to notify or report matters to the SRA is satisfied if the solicitor informs the firm's compliance officers.
- Ultimate responsibility for how a firm is run and the legal services it provides lies with its managers.
- Every firm must have compliance officers tasked with ensuring compliance with the SRA Standards and Regulations.

Sample questions

Question 1

A solicitor attends a private party at a friend's house. A good deal of alcohol is consumed. Tempers flare and the solicitor is caught up in a fight outside the house. The neighbours call the police. The solicitor is arrested for assault. The police decide to issue the solicitor with a caution rather than proceed with a prosecution.

Which of the following best describes how the solicitor's duties operate in this situation?

A The solicitor is not obliged to do anything as they have not been convicted of a criminal offence.

B The solicitor will meet all their duties by informing their manager about the caution.

C The solicitor is not obliged to do anything as the SRA will not consider this to be a serious matter.

D The solicitor is under a duty to notify the SRA about the caution.

E The solicitor is not obliged to do anything as the incident occurred outside the solicitor's practice.

Answer

Option D is correct. Paragraph 7.6 requires the solicitor to notify the SRA if they are subject to a criminal caution – a conviction is not required (option A is wrong). The requirement to notify the SRA in these circumstances is a strict one; the seriousness or otherwise of the matter is not relevant (option C is wrong). The duty applies irrespective of whether the offence occurs outside practice (option E is wrong). The solicitor could satisfy their duty by notifying the firm's compliance officers, not the solicitor's manager (which means that option B is wrong).

Question 2

A solicitor is acting for a defendant in a personal injury matter. The case is settled on the basis that the defendant will pay damages of £10,000. The solicitor undertakes that the £10,000 will be paid within seven days. The firm's policy is that when an undertaking is given, a written note must be placed on the client's file. The solicitor puts a written note on the file and then goes on two weeks' holiday. No one from the firm looks at the file in the solicitor's absence and consequently the £10,000 is not paid on the due date.

Which of the following best describes who has breached the SRA Codes of Conduct?

A   As the person who gave the undertaking, the solicitor alone has breached the Codes of Conduct.

B   The firm's managers bear ultimate responsibility and so they alone have breached the Codes of Conduct.

C   The firm's COLP bears ultimate responsibility and so they alone have breached the Codes of Conduct.

D   The solicitor is not in breach of the Codes of Conduct because they have complied with the firm's policy.

E   The solicitor, the firm and the COLP are all in breach of the Codes of Conduct.

Answer

Option E is correct. The solicitor is in breach of their duty to comply with the undertaking. The firm's policy is clearly inadequate. Whilst the managers bear ultimate responsibility for the firm's compliance with the Codes, such an inadequate policy places the COLP in breach of their obligations under Paragraph 9.1 of the SRA Code of Conduct for Firms.

Question 3

One evening a solicitor goes to a restaurant for a meal with various colleagues from the solicitor's firm. At the end of the meal, a colleague says that they have left their wallet at home, but the colleague is still able to pay their £100 contribution to the bill in cash. The following day the colleague tells the solicitor that a client had given the colleague £500 in cash as costs on account for the work that the firm would be doing on the client's case. As it was too late to give the money to the finance department, the colleague had kept the cash with them on their evening out for safekeeping. The solicitor queries the colleague using the cash, but the colleague insists that they were only borrowing the money.

What should the solicitor do?

A   The solicitor is not obliged to do anything as the colleague was only borrowing the money.

B   Report the matter to the SRA.

C   The solicitor is not obliged to do anything because £100 is only a small amount of money.

D   Tell the colleague to repay the money immediately.

E   Report the matter to the firm's compliance officers.

Answer

Option E is the best answer. This is a misuse of client money and as such is likely to be viewed as a serious breach of the regulatory requirements, irrespective of the amount involved or the colleague's intent. This is therefore a matter which the solicitor must report under Paragraph 7.7. The solicitor could report the matter to the SRA direct, however, the solicitor will discharge their duty if they report the matter to the compliance officers (Paragraph 7.12). This would be a better option as it would enable the compliance officers to review all the circumstances before, if necessary, formally involving the SRA.

Index